MW01096387

ONE

FROM

NONE

ROLLINS

ONE FROM NONE

Collected work 1987

SEVENTH PRINTING *©1993 2.13.61 Publications*

Cover Photo: Justin Thomas
Back Cover Photo: Steven Stickler
Layout & Design: Endless Graphics

ISBN # 1-880985-04-7

2.13.61

P.O. BOX 1910 · LOS ANGELES · CALIFORNIA · 90078 · USA

2.13.61 / ROLLINS Info Hotline #: (213) 969-8043

Thank you: Stan, Gary I, Lynn Nakama, Gail Perry, Robert Fischer, Mitch Bury of Adams Mass

Inspiration:
Ian MacKaye, Don Bajema, Hubert Selby, Jim Osterberg, Phillip Lynott, Bill Shields, Coltrane, Toshiro Mifune, James Marshall Hendrix, James Brown

Dedicated to John Macias
Shot and killed by 4 bullets to the chest and neck from the gun of a Santa Monica policeman May 31, 1991

JOE COLE 4.10.61 - 12.19.91

OTHER BOOKS FROM 2.13.61:

ONE FROM NONE

My mind is behind a locked door
I can't get out
I feel like punching my head in
I get mad at myself
All the stupid shit I get myself into
All the shit I have to take
I never get tired of it
I never get finished with being frustrated
I can't let go
No compromise?
Bullshit
I get compromised all the time
I do it to myself
I am weak
Everything that happens to me
I let happen
It's all in my head
I have killed myself a million times
I never get tired of killing myself
What a way to live
What a fool
   . . .

You can't hold me
Your tears don't imprison me
Your love no longer leeches my soul
Your love makes me hate love
In your eyes everything becomes a move
A sleight of hand
I don't have shit up my sleeve
I don't play games
I have a headache
My skull feels like it's going to come out of my mouth
And you ask
"What does that face mean, what have I done now?"
I feel like educating your face

I don't want to lose anymore of myself in you
  . . .
At the end of the line
I can see it now
All the things I felt so strongly about will be as they should
Mere trifles
All lovers will be childish cock meets cunt stories
I will know all people as they knew me
A liar
  . . .
At some point they show their true colors
After the break up
After the trial
After the contract is signed and broken
Their true colors stink
These days
I find it hard to get along with them
I want to push them until the colors come out
And sometimes I hate them so much, I push and see
I do the same to the ones I like
The ones I don't care about
I smile at real nice
  . . .
I closed my door
I saw the world frowning at me
I sat shut away from their downward spiraling universe
I stared at the walls
My universe frowned at me too
Shut away
Turn away
I want an eject button I can push
So I can get out of myself
When my universe frowns at me
  . . .
One ball hangs lower

Since I was 19
A bouncer tried to pull it off and take it home
He was real quick with that ball grab
Either he did it
A lot
Or had it done to him
Once
  . . .
Climbing the fire ladder
Burning fire house in the sky
The clouds part for me
My head full of insane
They let me in
because they know I come to drag the bodies away
And turn them into soft ash
Hot ladder rungs burn my hands
Warm my heart
Help me sleep
The night is the day burnt to a crisp
  . . .
I don't believe in opposites
Black the opposite of white?
Right the opposite of wrong?
No opposites in my mind
Free to think
Opposites divide
Opposites make the mind trip
No opposites in my mind
I see no opposition
  . . .
These train rides at night
Looking at the glass
Seeing myself
Trying to look thru
Seeing myself staring back

I can hear the whistle blow as we roll
Into Erie Pennsylvania
4 AM

. . .

We pulled each other close
I could feel her hips and breasts pushing against me
Her hair
Her eyes
Her lips
Her neck
She exhaled into my ear
I almost started crying
So long alone
At last, a real woman

. . .

I want to take a screwdriver
Mutilate my face
Find a beautiful woman
Make her love me for what I am
Then say I don't need it and walk away

. . .

Don't ask me about the rings under my eyes.
They're darker than yesterday
I just looked in the mirror
Ugly
Maybe I am dead and just dreaming of life
They don't know me

. . .

Got sick of sitting alone in my room
Got sick of spinning downward into the black hole in my head
Wanted to break off
Disengage
I turned around
Got hot
Got part Animal part Machine

Disintegrated into one
No more alone and lonely
Got myself all one and only

. . .

This train ride
That's all we got tonight
What a mean game to be left with
The lonely drunk man in the dining car
Cowboy hat and boots
Holding a Budweiser
Swaying with the train
Trying to start conversations with all that pass
Lonely cowboy
From nowhere
Heading to Chicago

. . .

I should have smashed that guy's head in
Straight shot no sound
Not even a thank you
All things all the time
War is my evolutionary process
Gets me from here to where I'll be
The next time I open my eyes
Holy man grenade launcher
I walk the line to paradise

. . .

Those people going to work are dead
Sure they are
That's the only way they could pull it off

. . .

The first day back is the hardest
When I get off the boat and see all this
I freak out
It's not paranoia
It's pig reality

When I get back here I think
I will never get back out there
I look out the window
I listen to all the talk
All I think about is getting out again
I wait
Simmering in the coat of a lie
I do my best to maintain
  . . .

I am sitting in this room losing it slowly
You know how it is
When nothing comes quick enough
And when it finally does, it's not what you needed
All the red lights in the world are flashing and nothing's right
Sometimes I can see myself swinging from a wire.
Face black, tongue sticking out
Making fun of me
  . . .

I was coming
I tried to push my back thru the hole in my cock
Bright lights
All things falling into perfect order
Dead bodies in piles
Total power
Full perfect war
So much incineration packed into seconds
Lots of flashing lights
All switches left on
The end of the world
Over and over
I tried to collapse my rib cage
I wanted to smash together
I wanted to feel the real force
It never gets real enough
I always want so much more

I want to see all things destroyed
To see all things come to an end
It's never enough and it drives me
Makes me want to chew my brain
To taste what I know
Makes me want to rip out my nervous system.
And see what I feel
It's never enough

. . .

They all look like hell jumped up their ass
They sit in the bus station
They drink and smoke and curse and hack
I can't tell if they're waiting for the bus
Or just waiting
Chicago Greyhound Station

. . .

That kid was on his way out
I watched him as we rode the train
Beer after beer
Didn't look like he was having fun
I heard him vomit in the toilet
I rode that train for 25 hours and got off
He kept going

. . .

All the things that matter
Take them away one by one
Burn them, sell them, I don't care what you do
Take all my things away from me
They hurt my eyes
Too easy to hang onto a lie
In my room I am a whole pack of goddamn liars!
I tell myself about the world I see thru my window
You should hear the things I say in here
If it all happened
A lot of people would be dead

I would be dead rich and mutilated
Hanging from an extension cord
Brains all over the wall

. . .

Memories don't hurt like they used to
Last year they cut and burned
It was my fault
I would go back and check on my memories
Like they were some kind of investment
When I would return to these places
To these people
I became lost inside
I think that people fear the fact that all things pass
All of a sudden you find
That you should have left the party a long time ago
All the great things that happened
Come back to make you feel crummy
You have to let go otherwise you get dragged
So many ways to burn out

. . .

Mister room
A big hollow animal
I sit in the belly and get digested
Your room and my room are the same
Sitting, waiting looking out the window
If you have one
(Hello cons, fight the power)
Telephone?
Hate it when it rings, hate it when it doesn't
The room is stronger than I am
Always here
It knows it's got me
I'm loyal to mine
Like making friends with the prison guards

. . .

I'm going to sit in this room until summer
It will be a great long wait
I am in cold storage.
I sit looking at the walls
Thinking about women, music and the heat
I want it all
I look out the window at the gas station
I try to imagine that I am somewhere else
Can't wait for the summer
A good chance to die

   . . .

Celine rocked like a motherfucker.
Goddamn!...they're dead!...walking corpses...and so young!...from
now on I push them all away...call me any damn thing you want...I
don't care!...they're dead, the pretty ones too!...so hard to talk to
them...a waste of time...so empty!... I can't figure out what makes
them go...too bad...life is over so quickly...oh well...I used to
care...things have changed and I see that I must have been out of
my mind to think that I could have woken them up!...they're
dead...can you imagine that...trying to wake the dead...what a
joke!...more powerless power to them!

   . . .

Think of all those people in their rooms
Lights off lights on
Sitting pacing screaming at the walls
Staring at them in clenched silence
Like a prison term
That's where I go
I get unhinged trying to deal with people
I feel like an idiot for opening my mouth at all
I sit in my room and play Black Sabbath records
I pretend that I am Bill Ward
I pound the air to Iron Man
And try not to break the typewriter
All the war vets in their rooms

All those who have been brushed aside
Thrown away shut down.
They know that the world is full of lies
Mean fragile and up to its teeth in death and bullshit
  . . .
They are unpredictable
I don't want to know what makes them go
  . . .
Obscure search for truth
Cutting thru a jungle full of lies and liars ·
I trip over vines
Cut my face looking around
I can see you though real clear
I'm always looking at you
Every move you make
All the ways you kill yourself
All the ways you run around
There's nothing here
Empty time spent passing empty time is making me insane
The truth is one person in a room
Looking out the window
Waiting on the storm
  . . .

No bullets in the chamber
The sound of my feet on the floor
Click
Click
No
Bang
  . . .
All my war stories are old
They hang like old clothes in the closet
No one wants to hear old war stories
It's all I have right now
My mouth flaps dry in the air

I am in this room pacing the floors
Sun up sun down grinding my teeth
Jumping at shadows waiting
I don't want to think about that old war any more
It's driving me up the wall with bad insanity
I need new war
High on war
. . .
All the beaten down men got on the bus long before I did
I look at their cheap clothes and run down shoes
Their bags of junk
Their faces look like they're going to drop off their heads
And hit the floor
Most of them are holding transfers
It's past midnight
They have a longer ride than I do
Makes me want to go to my father's house right now
And kick his ass for making me scared of him
I should have been scared of guys like these
That doesn't make much sense
But look at these guys riding into the night
Like a sad song played out of a cheap radio
. . .
I hate to feel need
I look at her and I need
I feel it burn
I have a black gift
I heal myself into a mass of scar tissue
Unparalleled in insensitivity
I numb myself to myself
Instead of listening to my need
I don't feel the cuts and I can't taste the blood
Like having a headache
Blowing your brains out to stop the pain
Stupid and gutless

But it's easy and it hurts so much
That it doesn't hurt at all

. . .

Stop the headache
Cut off the head
Stop the bleeding
Drain the body of blood
Stop the war
Kill both sides
Stop hunger
Starve them to death
Stop crime
Put everybody in jail

. . .

He sits in his room night after night
No one comes over or calls
He makes no sound
He looks at his hands
He looks at the floor
He listens to his breath
He doesn't look at the clock
Time doesn't matter
His hands don't matter
He doesn't matter
He pays no attention to his thoughts

. . .

I told this girl that I had a dream about her
She looked at the ground and was silent
I felt stupid
I did have a dream about her though
She was smiling in the dream
She didn't smile when I told her about it
I don't look for friendship in people
I know where I am
I know where I am with them

It hurts to feel like a stranger all the time
But if that's what you are, that's it

. . .

I had this dream about a girl, where I was trying to talk to her.
Every time I put my hand out to her, it would get out of control
and try to slap her. She kept backing away as I approached. I
tried to tell her that I was sorry but the words came out wrong.
Instead of something good, it was a threat. All of a sudden I
started kicking her. She ran away and I tried to follow her but
my legs wouldn't move.

. . .

Summer
Wild insane hot animal all the way live sweat propelled
War and sex for fun hanging in
Hanging on and swinging from it
Bullets blowing brains all over town summer
I promise you
I will be there

. . .

There were things I wanted to tell you
I couldn't get it together
I couldn't get past your eyes
After you were gone it hurt to have kept quiet.
So easy to keep quiet and not say what you think
Not do what you want
Hard to take rejection
Easy to hurt someone else and not know it
Easy to make it hard

. . .

They will try to destroy you
At all times on all levels
All the things that go bump in the night twist your balls
Listen to how they talk
Sounds like trash falling out of their mouths
Every sound, every motion wants a piece of you

You must:
Disown
Disavow
Discard
You must break it over your knee
Dislocate
Take a look around
Look at all the animals looking at you
  . . .
I sat in the front seat of her car staring at her eyes
They seemed suspended
The street lights made her hair glow
Her neck
Her chin
The small scar
The swell where her left breast began
Her collar bone
Her lips
I traced them with them my tongue
Sometimes I think that I am going to rip out of my skin
The smell
The taste
Makes me want to explode
Every pore cries out to me
Makes me want to be known
By only one person in the world
Makes me want to feel the need to want to feel
 . . . .
Back at the intersection
The dead girl lying on the pavement
The rain beating down on her face
I saw the guy who did it
He was standing next to his car
Looking like he was trying to answer a tough question
She knew what to do

She waited for the ambulance

. . .

You're lonely and you're waiting
You're in the cancerous arms of need
You think that you're dying
You are

. . .

They're all strangers to me
Sometimes I want to be known
I feel like I am at the bottom of a hole
I want to kick all the strangers
Inside
I fall into her eyes
Please know me
I am lost
I can't talk
I don't know
Please know me and understand

. . .

Thank you for letting me see you cry
Good to see you have a heart
You're real
Maybe we are not so far apart
Words can only get so close
The closest we get is so far away
It's the distance that hurts
The freeze out makes it worse
Your tears soften your face

. . .

They will try to destroy you
That's all I know right now
I go out and that's all I can see
Walking killer diseases
Fucking knife heads
Fear running wild

Seeing the real thing and calling it something else.
Walking away with ground staring eyes
Pretending all the way to the grave
Like they got 500 years to live
You will try to destroy me
If I'm not careful I'll help you
Like waltzing with a lie
Instead of walking with fire
Fuck it
I will crush you with my life
You are disease

. . .

I am the man in the frozen night cell
I am the man behind the shrieking red hot walls
Unhinged from the earth
My eyes are endless windows
All things compact and fall in
All the time I try to sweep my mind clean
The garbage piles up faster than I can burn it
In my room I am the bullet
I am the axis
I am the reason to pull the trigger
I am snapped off from the earth
I don't miss a thing
In my room nothing is missing
One of these days I will come to my senses
I know they're in here somewhere

. . .

In my hot room I am rising
I am a dead man right now
Come into my room and kick me
I need to feel you
I don't care how you do it
I need to feel
Touch me hard

Grab me
Shake my bones
I need to feel it
Shaking hot insane driven in
Pull me out
Pull me apart
I need it
Can't you hear the war sounds
The fire at our backs
Come into my room
In this lonely heat I am freezing
Burn me up
You know how to do it
Burn me beyond recognition
I don't want to know who I am
Turn me to ash
Burn me white hot
I don't want to see myself
You know me
Burn my flesh
Make me hear the animal sound
Destroy me
  . . .
I need something to kick
The animals are beating on my ear drums
I can't touch the madness that I crave
It dances in front of me
I am hungry for what will destroy me
I want it right now
I am the only animal in this room
Full of people
  . . .
I am close to no one
That's the way it is
I have no need to bleed for you

It doesn't feel good
Makes no sense.
I am not cold blooded
I am a stranger
I go so far and that's all you know
No one gets close to me
Walk away
Don't say a word
It's no use
Lies take up too much time
Too much pain already

   . . .

I chew holes in the fabric of creation
I am the survivor of the all night room
I don't look for ways out
I know where I am

   . . .

Soon I will be gone again
Another tour in the van
Today I wrote a list of the things I need to do
Before I get to get the fuck out of here
At the top I put:
Rollins-bailing man
Like Pere Ubu
Done it so many times now it's like breathing
The last few days are like countdown
Take a look around the small room
Enjoy the last few moments of clean and quiet
I am 26
I wonder how long I will be doing this for
I wonder what will stop me
Waiting to go is harder than the tour
Maintaining everyday
Listening to these people talk
Dealing with people who have no idea

I will be in shitty clubs the rest of my life
I feel at home in those dark shit holes
I will bury all these fuckers

. . .

I keep my madness to myself
It's all I've got
Your eyes don't do anything for me
When we go we're gone
I keep waiting for one of you to touch me
All you do is touch my flesh
I talk to you and I get so cold
Better than it used to be
Used to get all hung up on you
I won't play these fragile human games
You used to frustrate me with your shallow embrace
Now you don't make me feel anything

. . .

I am Death's custodian
I clean up after myself
And wait for death to blow out the flame
Death is inside me all the time
Like a friend but better
No lies
No judgement
The tap on the shoulder at the end of the trail
Death calls out in even tones
Everyday louder and sharper
The later days will be thunder storms
With my life I serve Death
The path is direct and I am on my way
The shortest distance between two points
Is the truth

. . .

I was walking
Up ahead there was a man

Hitting up people for change
He got to me and made his pitch
Hello my friend!
I could smell the booze on him
I need 25 cents for a pack of cigarettes!
He looks at the tattoos on my arms
Those ain't shit, look at these!
He shows me these burns in his arms
Geometric patterns
Now these are something!
I asked him if he got those in jail
No! I got these in college! Cleveland!
I asked him what class it was
That required such mutilation
He didn't get the joke
I gave him the quarter
Reminded him that smoking was bad for his health
He stuck out his hand to shake mine
He went into this intricate handshake routine
I didn't know what to do
He laughed
Said that my tattoos were bad
I said gosh thanks

   . . .

I could drown in her shallow eyes
I could feel like crust
But

   . . .

Beating off into the sink part whatever:
No one can touch me like I can
I learn about myself
Get stronger
Whoever said that shit about no man is an island
Has never met me

   . . .

Big Larry the black fag
We used to hang out at the Old Europe parking lot
I would watch him park cars
We would hang out on the avenue and talk
So much bullshit
Sometimes all we could do was laugh
He would sometimes reach over and grab my dick
I would say get off me you big black fag
We would laugh like shit
He would look at me with these watery eyes
He would say:
White boy, you got no box, you got no ass
What are you going to do?
I didn't know
I asked him why the hell he didn't like women
He laughed so hard he nearly fell of his crate
He said that there was something about that big old piece
Just hanging there, really did it for him
I told him that women were what was happening
He laughed hard as shit
Asked me how the fuck I knew that
I didn't know shit about women
Much less anything else
All I had was a milk crate under my ass
And this big black motherfucker
Grabbing my dick
I told him that I was with women all the time
He laughed so hard
I thought his eyes were going to fall out
Ok Larry, you're right again
    . . .
I am trying to solve this problem inside myself
I am too nice for my own good
Seeing the people that I have to work with
I should be a real fucker
So I can keep my head above water

I am working hard
Makes me mean as shit
Nice guys have a lot of friends
Then they fall and have none
They cry and wonder why
The friends you have when you're down
Are the only ones that matter
We have one thing in common
We have a lot less friends than we think

. . .

In my room, no eyes of the world upon me
No one to hear me, I am free
Hard to handle it out there
Hard to find a reason to go out
Into that screaming shit
In here I breathe easy
Soon the walls will close in
I will lose my smarts
I will leave to try to destroy it all
Sucker

. . .

I met a guy once
He had been locked away in solitary for a stretch
When they came to let him out, he didn't want to go
He liked it better in there
Said it was a world that he could understand and control
Sometimes I think it would be better to stay in a cage
It gets hard to take the shit that these fakes put across
They should be careful
Someone might take them out of the picture
Just for a laugh
Or because they have the blues
The world is big
You see how people react to the terror
The size and the noise
Freaks them right out

They wish for the cage like I wish for the cage.
Sometimes I want to kill you
Make you wish you gave me the cage
Before one of your pigs takes me out
I am going to take a few of you down
I have the blues from the size and the noise
Where's that cage

  . . .

It's hard to start this
I want to die in my sleep
Every thing I wake up, I stare at the ceiling
I think about my death
Tonight I was trying to sleep, I saw all the sad things in my life
All the things that I have attached myself to
Things that drag me into the darkness
We are joined
I used to think that I was followed around by it all
Now I see that I drag it along

  . . .

That girl fucked a dead man
Me
I don't remember a thing she said
I am dead
It doesn't feel good like it used to
It's a joke
A pack of lies
How do we keep pulling it off

  . . .

My skull
What a fragile house
No place for a brain
See the bald man on the bus in front of you
Would you like to smash his skull with a hammer
To see what was inside?
To see what was on his mind?
Might be good to go home tonight and pull my brain out

Throw it all over the room
Kick its ass and get it back in line
Been acting up lately
Looking for the on off switch
Looking for a good skull shredder
The thought that weighs a ton.
. . .
All things in war time
Straight line to where you need to go
All in war time
All this and so much more
Good time war time
Hello war time
What took you so long
Glad you're here
Now you're all I see
You are everything
That's how I will destroy you
. . .
She likes me too much
I like it when they like a little
I don't like anyone more than a little
She likes me more than I like myself
She makes me sick
. . .
I am the axis tonight
All things
Can't shut off my mind
Can't stop the eyes from seeing
The overload never comes
I become selfless
I do all things for no reason
No reason is the reason
All things tonight
. . .
The lies that come out feel good to say

Sound good to hear
Truth is sometimes painful
Sometimes people like to get out
There's always someone else who wants to get out
We find each other
We like lies

. . .

Walking on a dark street looking for a friend
Looking at the faces that pass me by
Wondering if anyone knows me
Someone without a hollow ringing smile
Someone that won't pass me by and ease the pain
I like the faceless faces
Perfect strangers in all the right places
Something to ease the pain
I have a long face
It falls to the ground
Looking for something to ease the pain

. .

We can get together
Talk, sing the old songs
We can keep each other's spirits up
After awhile it sounds real
We will believe it
With lies we can ease the pain
To kill the pain would be good
Looking for a way out of it
At the end of the night we separate
We becomes I
And then it gets real
That can be hard
The night gets cold
The emptiness so huge
The everything so all the time
That's why we cling
Like leaves to a shivering tree

Trying to hide from death
By running headlong into its mouth
  . . .
I can see why tigers jump thru rings of fire.
I can see why men jump thru penthouse windows
Poor tigers
  . . .
Gun in mouth blues
I am breathing in night air
I am going to take the big breath
This is important
The stars are in the sky
They shine like diamonds
Cold and far away like me
Like this whole fucking place
The walls are singing tonight
It's all coming to me
All things are compacting into one
Life is a joke
A tease
Now :
Shot in the dark
Knee jerk
Oily smoke
Brainless
Hot man
Filling the room
With the rising sun
  . . .
I have come back to you swinging man
I left you in that room years ago
I went out into the light and looked around
I have come back into the darkness
To bask in your rancid creaking rhythm
I can hear you swing back and forth
I can see liquid dripping from your mouth

Sticking your tongue out, making fun of the world
I see why now
They make me feel like they made you feel
Hollow and alone
Emptied and gutted
I must tell you right now
Silence is the most powerful sound I have ever heard
The things they said feel good
Don't
You could never fit in
So you made your own place
That's what I need to do
I feel pushed out of everything
I wish I could have seen you kick out the chair
It would have been great to see your eyes
But then again
That wouldn't have been too good for you
The best things are done alone

  . . .

Take my hand
Come into this dark room
Get down on the floor with me
Let's get slain
Lick the sweat
Taste the blood
Hear the sound
For once
For real
I need something real from you
I want you so bad
I want to taste you
I need to feel your teeth in my flesh

  . . .

F train
What do you mean she looks bad?
She sticks needles in her arm

That's how junkies look
Her face is wasted, she looks tired
I know, but look at her eyes
She looks like she is hanging on for dear life
She looks good for a junkie
She sucks a needle's dick
That's love in her eyes
Real love
She has that junkie glow
She looks good for a junkie
It must be hard to be one of those
I bet she fucks like a piece of wood
You think?
Yea man, she's a junkie
Look at her skin, man
Yea, she's fucking glowing
What a trip
Yea well I'd fuck her even if she is a junkie
Yea?
A fuck is a fuck, right?
I guess so, but shit man
You think she'll be alive a year from now?
I don't know, sometimes those junkies
They're like vampires or something
Yea, that's what she looks like
Here, throw this at her
No way, you do it
Ok
Shit did you see that, she didn't even flinch
She's creepy, like that bitch in the Addams family
Yea

            . . .

I took you to you
That's what you wanted
I think I did a good job
You got mad when I left you there

You cursed me
For the stench of your trash
Well, it's all you now
Sooner or later you'll see
The sun shines outside the sewer
It's easy to come away empty handed when you don't reach out
It's hard to believe you when you say you're choking
When you have your hands around someone else's throat
It's all you and you now
If you lean too far to one side you will fall
You'll have to pick yourself up off the floor of your soul
Scar tissue is stronger than normal flesh
It's all you for you now
All things inside
The poison
The medicine
All in you for you

  . . .

When I look at you
I want to destroy your smile
It sits on your face like a lie
You look good
I want to know the truth about you
I want to get close to you
When I do, you see that I see thru you
Your heart beats like a small bird
You know me well
That's why you can't handle me
It hurts me to act a fool
Pretend I don't see you for what you are
All of you keep me on the outside
I want to believe your lies
Turn myself off and feel you
But I can't stop seeing thru
All of you

  . . .

He sat in the dark room and waited for her
She was not his friend
He tried friendship for years and knew the truth
He wanted someone to be nice to him for an hour
He was lonely
It made no sense that someone would find him attractive
That someone would want to be with him for what he was
In his business everybody wanted something
There was always an ulterior motive, a game being played
There was something wrong when someone was nice to him
And they weren't getting paid
Every time someone wanted to shake his hand
He wanted to say:
What are you after
How much do you want?
He was not a bad person
He just couldn't identify
He sat and waited for her to come
She was a whore
Not off the streets, she was high class
His manager got her for him
There was a knock on the door
He opened the door and she came in
She looked at him and smiled
She looked down at a card in her hand
Asked if his name was Frank
He nodded
She went into a speech about the things she wasn't into
Rough stuff, anal sex, S&M
He nodded
He spoke:
It's hard for me. I'm not used to this. I need you to be nice to me
for awhile. I want you to pretend that you know me and like me.
You don't have to take off your clothes unless you want to. Maybe
you could just put your arms around me for awhile. Could you do
that for me?

She put her arms around him
He closed his eyes
He felt good
She looked over his shoulder at the television
She almost started to laugh out loud
She wanted to ask if she could light a smoke
What a crack up, this rock star
Her little brother had all of his records
If he knew what he was really like, he would throw them out
After a short time he pushed her away
Gave her a wad of money
Said: It's all there, thanks
Get out

  . . .

Warm salt girl
I can taste you
I can't get enough

  . . .

Don't talk to me about your training
What the fuck are you training for
There is a difference between making someone happy
And inflicting your happiness on them
Don't drag me thru your happiness
Your unhappiness was bad enough

  . . .

They don't lie a lot
They just don't tell the truth very often
Truth does not mean much to them
You can lie to them, or tell the truth
Makes no difference to them
Walk on them if you want
Eat with their forks
Destroy them for the hell of it

  . . .

War is all
Born into war

Live and breathe war
Life is war
No dead dreams in war
Life with urgency
War is beautiful
Real love
Real hate
All things taken all the way
War is holy
War is all
I am alive
I am at war
In war
From war
    . . .
He weighs 250 pounds
He beats her
    . . .
I am not in this room
I am outside
I am a million miles from right now
Breathing fire
Waltzing with shadows
Looking for death
    . . .
Animals in pain
Sweating and screaming
Bullets blowing brains across apartments all over town
The janitor hangs himself in the basement
Had a falling out with god
Leaves a note saying he was sorry for his life
She grinds cigarettes into her first born's back
Hot night breaks jaws
All is fair in love and hell
If you don't like it, crawl on your hands and knees
And stick your head in the oven

Breathe deep
Dying in rooms
Crying out from plaster tombs
Heroin worship
Nightmare in the womb
Sliding down the icy spike
No way but out
  . . .
Another gun in mouth blues
Another day, no answer
Fist thru the mirror
Fist thru the wall
Pull back
The pain
Over and over
Gun in hand
Itchy finger
Perfection
Pull back
Shut down
So far down
So far out
All the way
  . . .
Ok on my own
Around people, I come apart
Waste energy
Could have put it into the work
They will never understand you
Best to move silent and unseen
Like the wind
Like a disease
Like dreams
  . . .
Look at me
Look closer

You see the distance grow
It cools and widens
You see that we are ugly
There is nothing left but the truth
It locks you with cold lips
You feel the lump in your throat grow
You can't get farther away than too close

. . .

Fevered brain
Bad water in the river
Foul taste in my mouth
Bile spit taste of blood
My eyes feel warm in their sockets
Ugly mind
It's real
She said that she didn't think I was like this
You are everything you say I am

. . .

There are a few good times left
I drink from their streams
Like a parched soldier
I take their damp rags and wring drops into my mouth

. . .

This wonder
The uncompromising will to destroy
I turn to the wall
They all fall away
The feather people
Inhale
Exhale them right out of the room
They don't even know
What a joke

. . .

Your cocks and cunts don't mean shit to me
Everybody has one or the other
They all do something with them

Your ruined flesh is all the same
You must think you have something special down there
   . . .

I will endure
I will turn to stone
I will maintain
I freeze like ice
A bullet of thought
Ice cold reality
Straight and clear
Everyday I see it clearer and clearer
It compresses itself into diamonds in my brain
Elimination
This is beauty like I never knew
   . . .

Yesterday this guy came up to me, handed me a piece of paper
Said that years ago he had met D. Boon
And asked him to write something about me
I read it:
  "Hank and I are bros with different moms,
    and I love him a lot. Thanks -D. Boon"
The guy told me to keep it
Now it's night
I am sitting in some room, there is a lump in my throat
The fleas are hopping
It will be hours before sleep
   . . .

Electric gasoline napalm woman
Make my knees weak
Suck the air out of my lungs
Turn the lights on
Rip my head off
Tear me limb from limb
Show me
Breathe fire into me
Burn this world down

I am not afraid
Drink my blood and smile at me
Electrify, illuminate, personify, incinerate
You know what my name is
You know me
You know what I am talking about
I can tell by the way you scream
You know why I am here
You've been dropping fire in my dreams
. . .
When I go into the bathroom in this hotel room I want to die. I feel
ugly. I can see drops of my blood on the floor tile. The florescent
lights make my skin look dead. I want to be dead. The hotel room
is choking me, killing me. I want to die right now. I can hear the
television sets from the other rooms. I have to live thru all their
commercials. I want a gun right now. Get the lead out. I don't want
your help. I don't want anything from you. I have had enough of
you and all that you want to do for me, to me.
. . .
I kneel down on the floor of my room
I pull back a section of the curtain and look outside
Half an eyeful is all I can take
Every pig eye in every house tries to catch me
They're like an army of diseases
I pull away from the window, I've seen enough
I crawl on the floor to different parts of the room
Can't stand up
Snipers, fuckers, pigs, you never know
Steely sounds from outside
Traffic talk
Metal dumb animal suicide pain gibberish
Soon the night will come
I will be able to breathe again
I will pull into my head
The place where I fuck and kill them all
Where I destroy myself

Where I smash myself into a million pieces
Grow scar tissue
Stronger than ever
Doomed to endure and prevail
  . . .
Every minute I spend alone I get stronger
Every time I keep my mouth shut
Every time I masturbate instead of touching a woman
I do a good thing for myself
When I stop resisting reality
When I see clearly
I must feed myself to myself
I cannot be destroyed by outside forces
I must keep the blade sharp
I must be hard on myself
I must remain one
Nothing matters except
The uncompromising will to destroy
The forward roll of the square wheel
  . . .
I reach deep inside myself
I rip out a handful of bleeding crackling wires
I squeeze the juice out
I burn them out
I want to see where the truth lies
I want to see where it all breaks down
I walk down the mouth of every beast I can find
So I can see what's at the end
That's the only part that interests me
The end
The rest is all getting there
  . . .
Sometimes while playing
Too much heat, too little air
The end of each song forces me to my knees
I reach for the water and try to breathe

When the last song has finished with me
I go staggering outside for real air
As I walk I think about how funny it is
One minute I am in the middle of hot lights and strangers
The next I am on some street with all the air I want
Feeling like I could do it over again
I get one sliver of relief
I wrap it around me like it's some kind of badge
Happens every night the music tries to kill me
. . .
Some nights it hurts so much to play
Every song hurts
Knees, back, head
No air, lungs searching
Hurts more every year
Good
. . .
Sitting on the sidewalk after playing a show where there was no air,
just heat and a room full of animals feeling free. Steam is coming
off my body even though it's June. A puddle of sweat is forming
around me. I hold a pitcher of water, it's all I need right now. They
start walking by. They stop to look at me. I can see their feet and
shins. I feel like a wax statue in a museum.
Hey
What
You guys going to Europe?
Yeah
When?
Next month
How long?
Three months
Tired?
Yeah
Hot in there
Yea
Well I thought you guys sucked

Uh
Hey
Yea
How do you feel?
Tired
Come over here these people want to meet you
I am tired, I am going to sit here, if you don't mind
Too stuck up buddy?
Whatever you say
Later
Hey
Yea
I really liked it tonight
Ok
You guys were cool
Ok
I am glad I came
Good
I really enjoyed it
Ok
Really intense
Ok
Tired huh?
Yes
Later
Hi my name is Ann
Hel-lo
I know your name already
Shucks
Could you introduce me to the singer in the other band?
I think he got hit by a truck
Ok, nice meeting you anyway
Sure

. . .

Every night I play I get harder
I can feel it

The sweat draws my pores closer together
I become stronger
After I play
I am complete
I need no one
I want nothing from the humans
I am night iron
I am the one

. . .

My head is shaved
All the scars show
The girls don't talk to me
I look in the mirror
I am ugly as shit
I looked better a few years ago
I am getting older and it's starting to show
I play music and throw myself into bad places
I do it in front of strangers who know my name
We have a good time
I sleep on floors
I beat off every few nights
I sleep alone
I am Part Animal
Part machine

. . .

Don't look at me
Don't talk to me
Don't touch me
I don't want to know your name
You think you have something that I want
You don't
I don't wait for you or your kind
You get mad
When one of them isn't killing themselves to be near you
Not everyone is so easily amused by biological functions

. . .

Don't ask me how it was
Don't ask me what it was like
Don't try to identify
Get the hell out of here before you get hurt

. . .

I was kissing her
Running my hands on her body
She wouldn't look at me
She stared at the wall
I removed myself
I apologized, I didn't know what else to do
She shrugged, put her clothes on
She turned on the TV and lit a cigarette
I never wanted to touch anyone again
Not even myself

. . .

Together
Two strangers
Clawing each others flesh
No words
Waiting room eyes
Dry mouth
Dry everything

. . .

Putting my arms around her was like hugging a mannequin
In a subway car

. . .

I touch her
Doesn't matter who she is
Feels the same
Tastes the same
Makes me empty

. . .

I know what I am
I'm ugly
I'm invisible to kind eyes

Untouchable like some kind of twisted gem
I'm a box falling into a hole
Passing thru unknown
They can't take anything from me
They don't make me feel anything at all
  . . .
Crawl to me
Get in line
Bend over
Swallow
Take it day in day out
Breathe in breathe out
Breathe no fire
Dead dreams but no fire
Kill yourself
Get up do it
Turn it on turn it off
Bend yourself into a shape
Dead room death row
Empty headed hollow man
Spinning hanging choking
Get up and do it become it live it
Believe
  . . .
Curling up and dying inside
Crawling into a corner because I know no one will be there
All the bad trips in your mind
All the asylum sweat
No mirrors in my room
I don't want to see myself
Endless time spent trying to destroy time
Crawling on the floor waiting for something to end
All the dying time in my room
  . . .
You have a lot less friends than you think
Out of nowhere a beautiful woman comes up and says hello

Startled the hell out of me
I smiled I couldn't believe this is happening to me
I say hello
She asks if she can be my friend
I say sure
She says I can be her best friend for 25 dollars

. . .

I must be terminally ill crazy or worse
Sitting here and can't find sleep
I am the all night man
I need to sleep so I can go to work tomorrow
I guess I don't care
Or I hate myself so much I want to fuck up
It's 3:30 in the morning and already it's getting hot in the room
Can't sleep in this room anyway
Always think that someone is going to come in and shoot me

. . .

I am the ice cold reality I have shoved down my throat
For the millionth time
Trying to survive
Lock and load in your brain
I am your mirror man
I have nothing else to breathe for

. . .

In the morning I felt stupid and cold
I didn't want to ask her what her name was again
We both laughed after she said
Will I see you again?
She said she was only joking anyway

. . .

I've grown
Violent
Intolerant
My goodness
Look how I have grown

. . .

Beating off into the sink
Cock in hand
Come!
Look into the mirror and see Superman!
Kind of

. . .

Some people don't need much to live on
Hell some folks live on pennies a day
I was right about to wrap my arms around that girl
But at the last minute
I jumped back and wrapped them around myself

. . .

Sometimes I feel so nice
Jump back, I want to kill myself

. . .

What's the matter, are you burning out? Are words failing you, things not like they used to be? Funny taste in your mouth, eyes hurt, life feels like a square wheel that's crushing you under its tread? Feel like your brain is dripping out of your ears? Feel like your face is going to slide right off your face? Do you think about death and when it's going to come to you? Do you think that your life is coming to a grinding halt while it's moving too fast to even understand it before it's all gone rushing past? It's a wonder the sidewalk doesn't swallow us whole.

. . .

I am tired of the fragile lies
That keep you alive

. . .

Downward into silence
Downward into darkness
I am falling into myself
I can see my skull shattering
Falling inward
I am caving into myself
The pieces fall to the bottom
I sit here and stare at the ground

I can feel it
I don't want to stop it
It's what had to happen
It is the ending place for me
Here in me

. . .

I must remember to punish myself
For all the time I waste on others
I should punch myself several times a day

. . .

If they asked themselves all the questions that they ask me, then
they would know something. If they had to deal with what they
make others deal with, then they would learn something.

. . .

I am the only one who can fix me when I break down
If I can't fix me then all is lost
I wish this weren't true
So many times I wished for the mercies of a woman
To heal
To take the pain away
I read about it somewhere
Tried it a few times
Too much pain
My instinct is to reach out
I see now that instinct is not always right
It hurts

. . .

I have to talk myself out of suicide tonight. Write myself away from
it. I want to hang myself from my chin up bar. That would be so
perfect. What a clown. Out of nowhere my fail-safe switches on. I
remember what I am, Part Animal Part Machine. I see that I have
to get into machine mode to get thru this shit. Part Animal, Part
Machine maintains me. Gets me to the next sunrise.

. . .

My brain is criminal
It runs from me

I chase
It hides like a fugitive
I want my thoughts back
It treats me like I am the enemy
  . . .
It's funny
These people try to bum me out
Calling me shit
They're not telling me anything I don't already know
When they talk shit
It's light weight compared to what I say about myself
They will never be as hard on me as I am on myself
So fuck them
Love me hate me, it's all the same
  . . .
Back in LA sitting on the front porch
Taking in all the smog
I must have forgotten how fucked up this place is
Those helicopters, they're like the state bird
Every time they go I flip them off
Maybe one day those little pigs will see me
Dive bomb the house and kill me
I always think of heat seeking missiles
Wouldn't that be great
Have a pick up truck
With a rocket propelled grenade launcher in the back
And a five cd changer in the front
Loaded with Black Sabbath
Cruising the blvd.
Hot woman in tow
Smoking those lawmen
  . . .
6.29.87 Silverlake California
Been home four days now
Feeling useless
What did I expect when I got back here

I always forget how empty and small this still life can be
Been here four days and I can't remember any of it
It's like I've been dead
Hard to sleep
Nothing makes sense except to leave again
The phone is ringing
Let it ring
I don't want to talk to them
    . . .
There was nothing in here tonight
I sat in this room and waited
Death did not come
A couple of weeks ago I was in Florida
Riding down a road, looking at the Everglades
Smelling the rotting swamp
Everything was alive and moving
Including me
I am a dead battery now
A shell for past experiences
An almanac
A reference book on what was and how much it hurt
I am an old war story
If I could have the big wish come true right now
I would want an enemy to embrace
Anything but this unchanging stillness
    . . .
In New Jersey she said:
  "Its always been a dream of mine to have you inside me"

In Rhode Island 6 people came and no one clapped

In Pittsburgh she said:
  "You're the most gorgeous man I have ever seen"

In Minneapolis the pigs arrested Joe

In Des Moines she said:
  "Its so exciting when you come inside me"

In New Brunswick he said I was a hippy

In Birmingham he said I was
  "A talentless jerk that stole freely from bad sources"

In Madison she said I was a typical asshole

In Washington I quoted Hitler and made her cry

In Athens I tried to fuck behind the police station

In St. Louis she said that she hates all men

In New Orleans he said that someone was coming to kick my
ass

In Pensacola she walked away from me, wordless

In Daytona beach she said I was a pig

In Miami bugs crawled on my face and I couldn't sleep

In Jackson she said:
  "Its hot and things move slow around here, that's why we
fuck a lot fight a lot eat a lot and drink a lot"

In Philadelphia I fucked in a men's room stall

In Columbia he said: "White power alright" I said: "Heil
Budweiser"

In Vermont I saw him get hit by a car

In Albany I saw him get taken to the loony bin

In Boston she said that her friend hadn't washed her shirt
since I sweated on it

In Lincoln 20 people came and they all sat in back or left early

In Memphis he pounded the stage with his brass knuckles

In Hoboken I spat puke for the last 3 songs

In Chicago I spat puke for the last 4

In Cincinnati I spat blood

Here in LA I wait to go
  . . .
Sometimes I have to ask myself
Am I feeling no pain, or am I numb
Am I suffering from burnout or bliss
Hard to make the distinction between satisfaction
And being too tired to argue anymore
I find refuge in the hot night
Sleepless dreams
Long drives
It's a strange peace
I can see myself clearly
  . . .
People get lost
The alarm clock goes off and someone loses their way
All of a sudden five years have passed
Same job
They look at themselves in the mirror
Can't understand where it all went
A dirty underhanded trick
Someone gets lost and destroyed

People walking the streets like dumb animals
Smart enough to be cruel
Handcuffed to the television set
Another beer can opens
The sun goes down on another day
Self destruction slow and complete
What nasty things we do to ourselves

. . .

Do you ever get the feeling that when you show someone your affection for them, you are assaulting them, like you should probably leave them alone? Your affection, no matter how sincere, does not necessarily mean a damn thing to the person you are giving it to. Love can corner you. When you intrude on someone with your affection, you might find yourself trying to knock a door down with your shoulder. Either you break the door or you break your shoulder, something almost always gets broken. In my mind it runs like this:
I'm going to like you, whether you like it or not
I'll wear you down
Until you relent and swallow this big lie I have for you
Don't move
Don't live
I love you

. . .

Tell me when to stop
Tell me when enough is enough
I don't understand
Don't let me hurt you
Sometimes I go too far

. . .

This cold box sterile room
The very thought makes me weak
The disease crushes me in its fist
The naked girl next to me
A lie
She makes me feel weak

No, worse
I find an excuse for my weakness in her eyes
I do all the bad things to myself
I try to blame them all on someone else
I am too smart for that now
In here I waste away
My soul atrophies
I need to be in front of something that's trying to destroy me
I want to destroy it, whatever it is
In here I destroy myself
That's what weakness and disease is all about
I should know
　. . .
She has brown skin
Dark brown nipples
Blue eyes
She smells good
She tastes good
She drives me wild
　. . .
What's it like to die
What's it like to come back to life
What's it like to be on fire
What's it like to break thru
Ask Selby
　. . .
I get calls from crazy girls
Late at night
They sound like they're calling from another planet
The other night one calls from some bin in O.C.
She tells me that her parents put her there
They no longer want to see her
Her older brother told her that she is ugly
She believes him
She starts to cry
She says that he goes out with a girl that got named

Ms. Huntington Beach
She asks me if she is ugly
I tell her she's not ugly at all
She says that her brother is a big fan of mine
And he wouldn't believe that we are talking right now
She tells me that she lives in a ward
A lot of other kids around her all the time
A tough weird reality
Almost 13 years old
She asks if she can call again some time
I say sure
She says goodbye and hangs up
I stare at the ceiling and try to fall asleep
I feel so lonely right now

. . .

1:22 AM
Phone rings
Long distance
She is off medication
Nervous about starting up with the new shrink
Trying to get her friends off drugs
"She works her ass off all week, gets her pay on Friday and it all
goes up her nose, she's trying to quit but it's hard."
She says that all of last year she was on medication
She sat in her room and stared at the wall
Her family pretended that she wasn't there
She goes to bars to be around people
She can't be alone for too long or she starts to slip
She says she is coming out to LA
She sounds like she's talking in her sleep
I tell her that I have to get up in a few hours
She gets mad
She tells me that I'm trying to avoid her
She calls me a few names and hangs up
Another night warped

. . .

She calls me from a bin out in the sticks
Tells me all about getting strapped down
Tells me that she's getting better
She can't feel it now
But they tell her that she's getting better all the time
I think of her as she speaks
Shitting her pants
Men in smocks putting electrodes into her head
I think about lab rats
The smell of shit
All these people getting better
Bright lights
White sheets
This stranger
　. . .
A girl called me once
Told me about her times in the home
One morning she woke up and saw a girl hanging
Her urine in a puddle
She said that she better hang up
If she didn't she wouldn't be able to stop talking
And it gets her upset
　. . .
Three pigs had me in the shadows
Rainy night in Santa Cruz
They wanted to work me over
I saw one of the pigs getting his gloves ready
He didn't ask any questions
I tried to steer the pigs to the street light
I wanted there to be some witnesses
Someone would get to see a guy in gym shorts
Standing in the middle of pouring rain
Get his ass kicked by a pig
Did you hit her?
No
Are you sure you didn't hit her?

I looked over at the pig with the gloves
He was on his toes
He wanted me to say yes so bad
No
He looked so let down
Like a child with a broken toy
I kept him in the corner of my eye
You never know when a pig is going to cheap shot you
They let me go
That's another reason stockpiled on a mountain of reasons
Why I laugh when I read about a pig getting killed
Imagine one of those pigs dying while a Crip laughs
Beautiful
I think it's wonderful
Like flowers and puppies and peace and love
And Hallmark greeting cards, frisbees, picnics,
Music and a pile of dead pigs burning
Whoa yea baby, rock and roll all night long

. . .

I thought you were really great up there tonight
- thanks
You're very intense
- thanks
I like the way you move up there
- ok
Are you in a bad mood or something?
- no
You look mad
- I'm not mad
What's the matter, don't like talking to girls?
- I got no problem with girls
Well, I just wanted to say that I really like what you do and that's
all. I'm not a groupie. I know you probably get a lot of girls back
here that want to fuck you, but I'm not one of those do you
understand, I'm only back here to tell you that I think what you do
is good, not great but good. I mean some of it I thought was shit but

the stuff that I liked I thought was good you know what I mean, I mean god, it can't all be good can it. You know, just because I'm a girl doesn't mean that I automatically want to fuck you
- yes, ok
Where are you going after you leave here?
- I don't know, probably some place to sleep
I'm not a groupie you know
- yes, I really believe you, I swear
I mean I don't even like you. I never heard of you before tonight, my friend has all of your records and told me to come here with her. I didn't want to come but I figured I would keep her company, you know, she's the one that wants to meet you, not me, she's too scared to come back here, but I wasn't, I mean you're just a guy, why the hell should be afraid of you?
- yes I agree with you, tell your friend that I'm glad that she enjoyed the show and tell her hello from me
Can I have a handshake? I mean god, I don't want to kiss you, how about a handshake
- sure, push it up there buddy
You're weird, are those tattoos real?
- hell no
I didn't think so
-I can fool a lot of people but not you, that's for sure
well, you sure didn't
- have a safe trip

. . .

Be careful of people
People on their way up
People on their way down or out
These punk rockers turned stoner record executives
So funny that they survive
Watch out for people who want to help you for no reason
Everyone is out for something
Watch your ass
People are everywhere

. . .

She makes me feel invisible
When I touch her and she looks at the wall
I feel like I am not there
Her face holds no expression
Every once in awhile she smiles
I hang onto the sparks
The light in her eyes makes me forget the blank moments
When she makes me feel like a piece of furniture
I am leaving her
There is one place for me
The road is always there for me
My endless friend
I will die on your shoulder
No woman will ever understand me
I won't waste my time with it
The road waits to destroy me

. . .

Thru insanity I will reach clarity
Watch me burn down the world
A fire dance
The only song
Me, trying to push it over
Trying to find out where it lies

. . .

To see I must push
I must smash my hand
Thru this brittle glass roof
To see I must
Destroy
Relentlessly
My thirst must be unquenchable
My hunger endless

. . .

Every time I beat off I get stronger
Every time I make myself come I love myself more
A triumph

I don't need them
I don't need to do that dance
I don't need to say those jokes
I don't need to lose sleep over some fucking stranger
All the beautiful women I see
Are just people walking down the street
The veil of mystery falls away
It feels good not to want anything
It's good medicine
I run the risk of becoming addicted to myself
The less I need, the more I am

. . .

I am one
Not five, not six
Lights flashing
Blinking eyes
Hiding lies behind smiles
You can't break me
You can't divide my strength
You must realize I won't break down
Got no half life
I got one life
Got no unity
I got me
I am one
Not 2 not 88 not 30
I am more
I am one

. . .

Bar 1
Swirling barroom scene
Sitting in a corner watching it revolve around me
When I look at them I feel the sun rising in my eyes
Living their lives away
Makes me want to be a human air strike
Look at those faces

I can't take it
The time to move is now
Everything they touch turns to plastic
. . .
Bar 2
Activate destruction
Move efficiently thru them.
Each footstep like the revolvers cylinder takes a footstep
Insulated self possession
Destroy with direct action
Go to the end
End it with ashes
I take a look around this barroom
Move
Destroy
March
Iron
Tranquil
. . .
Bar 3
Why are you alive
In my world you couldn't last
You fuck
Weak piece of shit
Let me help
Let me take the pain away
. . .
I am exploding
Burning holes thru my skull
Bright light
Hot night light
Ripping thru my room
. . .
After this is over I will return to a small dark room
I will sit and stare into the darkness
No one will come

No one will touch me
There will be no calls
My life is a hollow scream
My memories no longer haunt me
They have been exterminated
My present reality is wreckage
That will take me the rest of my life to pull out of
. . .
Don't look back
All memories will try to kill you tonight
. . .
I am in myself
All the way in down and thru
I sleep with myself
I feed myself
I fuck myself
I hear what they say
Strangers have touched my flesh
Made me want to destroy it
Sometimes it all seems so alien
I turn on myself
I try to hurt me
I should know myself better by now
I don't
I hear the things I say
Makes me want to turn around and say
Who said that?
Sometimes I want to end myself
I get trapped and scared
Cornered in my corner
I get revenge on myself
I can smell myself
I want to turn myself off right now
Lose myself
Hide from myself

A tragic summer holiday

. . .

I will make black music all night long
I will scream in the dark
I will go deep into the night
As if the rising sun would incinerate me
Which it has before and will again
Destroying my black music
Incinerating my black night dreams
Making all my words unspeakable

. . .

For some there is no music
No lights
No fire
No untamed madness that breathes life
There is work
Anguish
Frustration
Rage
Despair
A dullness that rings like wooden thunder

. . .

I saw myself in the sky tonight
Hanging suspended by life
Distant
Shining alone
Free and cold

. . .

I shoved my existence down my throat
Pushed it like a shopping cart
I want to see what happens
I want you to see what happens

. . .

Sometimes I think that my skin will rip open
My eyes will fly out of my face

My brain will rip out of my skull
Smash thru the ceiling
I will get real nice
Settle down with a girl
And start shooting pig bitches like you in the head

. . .

You're going to look good after the car crash
It's coming you know
I remember you told me once
-You're going to be great in five years
Thanks
But you're going to die soon in a car wreck
You've got nice eyes and you taste good
I can see your crushed body plain as day
You in the body bag
All that blood
Those hips crushed to jelly
Hey jelly roll
That's rock and roll talk you stupid bitch
Don't worry about it
You're good as dead
I'll do it
I'll come down to the morgue and identify you
It's been awhile since I've seen you
What the hell
I have been putting in a lot of time here you know
Trying to burn out parts of myself
Customizing my mind
Soul amputation
I was given much too much
My goal is to see a stranger in the mirror
The last time I saw you, we were fucking
I looked into your eyes
I knew you were going to be dead soon
You had the look of a loser
I knew you were going to get broken

. . .

I've got only so much
So I am using it
I can only do so much
So I'm doing it
I am on fire
I am burning out
While I burn
I burn brightly
My war will end

. . .

I am in my room
Pacing back and forth across the floor
I can hear water dripping off the pipes
I can feel the hair growing on my face
I want to come out and kill your kind
I want to put my tongue in your mouths
I turn and look at the wall
I see my face reflected back at me
The music in my head is driving me insane
Do you ever feel like dying?
All the time I want to destroy myself
Sometimes the only thing I love is my death
Thinking about it
Knowing that I can terminate myself
Makes me feel almighty
I keep it under control
To maintain is to prevail
I need to keep my self control
I have lost too much already
I hear the distant rain
I wait
My hands turn to fists and back again
I know it can't go on like this

. . .

It is violent summer in my brain

Napalm summer rain inside
The sound is getting so loud
Exterminating parts
The signal so clear
The light so bright
In the distance
The sound of animals dying
Important famous deadly sounds
An evil siren singing to me
It's all unraveling
One more night of this prison and then it's freedom time
. . .
Alone is best
Better than women
Why bother
At the end I am alone anyway
That tells me everything
There is no strength in numbers
Listening to them talk is depressing
Better off alone in the soldier brain
In my man hole
All these tours push farther into myself
They're all strangers
It's cold everywhere
You look for warmth in their eyes
You get stung hard and dropped
I am better off alone
The other pain is a lot worse
. . .
After show Sweden:
Don't talk to me
Get your stink breath out of my face
I don't want to hug your drunk ass
I could break this room over my knee
. . .
After the show I wanted you so bad

I licked the sweat off my arms and pretended it was you
I had to rip myself away from that thought
It was like trying to tear a brick in half
    . . .
Some nights I look into their eyes
I see rows of empty houses
The trail is endless friendless and full of lies
Ice cold places, vacant faces
I had to get away from their leeching complacency
Or explode completely
Self expression, they can't touch it
Their dead hands can't pull it down
It's a mute lesson that screams
A vision that blinds
A heat the freezes
A fulfillment that empties and leaves me with myself
Again and again
I can't get enough
    . . .
I went for a walk
Tried to lose my troubled mind
I've got a troubled mind
It sits in my skull like a frozen rock
I've got to lose my troubled mind before it rips me apart
It gives me a thousand ugly faces
Makes me say all the wrong things
Makes me wonder if I am dead
It has a mind of its own
Makes me think I've got lead running thru my veins
I walked and walked
Went thru alleys and backstreets
Tried to lose my troubled mind
    . . .
There are dark and cold times you have to stumble thru alone
There are days when there's not a cloud in the sky
But when you look out the window you see rain falling

There are times when the leaves are sitting still on the trees
And you would swear you were in the middle of a storm
You look in the mirror
Wrap your arms around yourself
And you don't know if you're there at all
The most simple things cause torment and confusion
All the lines run together
You look for the closest hole to fall into
This is when you must remember what you are
You must get back to the real number
You are a number
The number is one

. . .

I want to shoot myself in the head
My body doesn't want to go on
I'm tired of the voices in my head
I can't look at these people anymore
Life's wheel is crushing me
The sun brings me no joy
I can't feel the difference in the seasons
I don't love anyone or anything
I'm not lonely
I want to shoot myself in the head
Kill these thoughts

. . .

I am the reason
I am the bullet
I am the number one
Tearing a scar in the sky
You should have seen them screaming and hitting me
My eyes were ripping holes in the rafters
They can't touch me
They don't know me
They can't ride with me
They can't destroy me
I've got a limp and an inside mind

Attitude armor with all my teeth jammed together
After the show I was in the shower trying to beat off
Nothing happened
I had to laugh
I'm dying piece by piece
Dancing like a dirty shadow in the chicken lights
The roar in my ears
War is all
It defines me
I have my good times
Crawling thru the wreckage
I have my bad times the rest of the time
        . . .
It's over
The jewels in your eyes have turned to coal and died
When I touch you I lie to myself
When we are together we are dead
We are rag dolls
Nothing to say
We walk hand in hand with a lie
Trying to be as deaf dumb and blind as we can
Kissing each other with razor lips
Sticking knives into desperate flesh
Making the pain mean something else
Ignoring the blood
It's over
It's dead
        . . .
You been having some good times?
That's great, tell me about it
No really, I want to know
I'm in a bad place right now
I'm having some bad times
It's cold grey and raining where I am
It would be good to hear about someone beating the rap
        . . .

Broken apart man
Put your fist thru glass
The pieces on the floor
That's me
I'm your man
Don't touch me

. . .

On the road I beat off
Toilet stalls, hotel showers, etc.
I don't touch women
Takes the edge off
I will not be distracted
I am not on tour
I am tour
Fierce
This is what's real and good
Every night a test of will
These fuckers
I destroy them
I hate life
I live to destroy it
Wear it out and make it scream

. . .

Falling down inside myself
In a hotel somewhere in Italy
Small room, traffic sounds
Suck the thoughts from my mind
When I close my eyes I can see the hole

. . .

Looking at women in fashion magazines
I like the pictures
They don't lie
I lie to myself
I can stare as long as I like
I won't get arrested
I won't have to break some boyfriend's face

They stare right thru me
Cold and distant
Just like in real life
It's as close as I want to get
I got nothing to say to them
I don't have to talk to pictures
Don't have to pretend
Don't have to be full of shit

. . .

Drove into Milan Italy today
Looked out window at another filthy city limit
Wondered how many had passed before my eyes
The dirt and the poverty doesn't faze me
They have quite the opposite effect
The garbage and the stench are the welcoming committee
I enter these places life a knife
I exit like a bullet leaving a skull
In between I walk trails thru their guts

. . .

I've been stuck with bad nights where all I could do
Was keep my brain from running down my neck.
I've been held down in dirty cities
The air burned my lungs
The food made me swear off food
Reduced me to a figure of fun
I've been thru eyes and ears
Assholes, keyholes, broken noses
Vomit, sweat, blood and alienation
On and on, over and over
I am stuck with my understanding of all this
At least I'm not stuck with you

. . .

Nowadays when some asshole in the crowd hits me, I fire on him
so fast I don't even remember what happened. My hand is pulling
back. I don't feel anything for the assholes that antagonize me. If
they go home after the show and find their families murdered and

their houses burned to the ground, I wouldn't bat an eye. People should be destroyed. Human garbage. Disrespect is a two way street.

. . .

Fat drunk brain dead Italian punker
Oh man fuck you
I see you looking at me with your hard ass stare
Like you got something
You make me laugh
Sitting here in this rancid shithole
You punk rockers are pathetic shit bags
Beer cans all over the floor
Stupid ass graffiti on the wall
Looking at me like you're so hard
I've been in shit holes that make this look like paradise
Don't lay your luke warm vibe on me
I'll break it in half and shove it up your ass
I'll endure anything you got
You might be a punk rock faggot
But you're not a human cockroach
So go fuck yourself punk

. . .

Every night I spend in these stinking shit holes
I get stronger
Hot nights, no air, tasting my own puke
Listening to strangers telling me what to do
Hitting me, grabbing my dick
Spitting on me, throwing cups of urine
You think that makes me want to curl up and die?
I get stronger
No weak ass piece of shit with a mouth and an attitude
Can fuck with me

. . .

What's inside must come out
I can't help it
I can't keep my mouth shut

These things burn inside me
Makes me scream out loud
What's inside must come out or I will explode
  . . .
Past midnight
Walking down a street in Vienna Austria
I saw a whore standing against a wall
Hips out, shoulders back, headphones on
Staring straight across the street
I walked by and gave her a wave
Her eyes bored right thru my pointy head
I kept walking thinking how tough and awesome she was
Three short Asian men passed me and went over to her
I hid in a doorway to watch
They looked her over
It looked like Snow White and the Three Dwarfs
But more fucked up
She stood there looking over their balding heads
Like they weren't there at all
They took a few steps back and held a short conference
They came back and one of them spoke to her
I saw her laugh
They walked away fast
What the fuck you shits
What do you got
Nine inches between the three of you?
Yea, I'll do all three of you
No sweat
What's the matter
You scared of a little pussy?
You fucking runts, get the fuck out of my face
I watched for another minute
She adjusted her headphones
And returned her gaze to the street
  . . .
By the train station in Vienna

White boots
Turquoise spandex covered legs
White panties worn on the outside
Riding on narrow hips
White top
Nipples pushing out against the cold Austrian night
Blonde hair
Beautiful face
High cheek bones
Cruel mouth
Eyes that could peel paint
Muscles and sinew
Stunning to my eyes
Out there on the street flexing it
Taking on the whole world with her ass
I wanted to bow
I wanted to kiss her feet
I wanted to tell her that I thought she was beautiful
That I wished more women had the balls to stand up
That's what I like
Women that aren't afraid to walk upright
I like women that are loud and profane
Alive
That whore
What pure violence in her eyes
Someone on the planet that isn't full of shit
. . .
Letter from Vienna 9.28.87 :

Hi, I'm writing you from Vienna, I remembered you talking
about Austria once. Made me think of you. In some nasty district,
it's a night off tonight so we have been left to our own devices.
Playing tomorrow night, have not played Vienna since 1983 when
Black Flag played here with the Minutemen. Just left Yugoslavia,
that was wild, everything there is clean and in order but there's
something unsettling about the place, I don't know what it is. I
hope this gets to you ok. The tour has been good. So far we have

played Sweden, Denmark, Germany, Switzerland, Spain, Italy and Yugoslavia. After this show in Austria, we go to Hungary I think, I don't look at the schedule anymore, I just play. Seen a lot of wild shit in the last two months. Tour is almost over, soon it will be time to go back to LA and do the phone hustle. Saw a lot of great scenery over the last few days, all kinds of mountains and lakes, all that postcard looking shit. Touring makes me nasty, it's hard to be cool to these people all the time. They can be very demanding. Broken English is hard to understand, hard to deal with after a show when I'm tired. But people are really into the band and that's great.

You know, these hotel rooms are depressing. The room tonight looks like a shooting gallery, there's all these fucked up looking guys burning out in the lobby. There's a pool of dried blood in the corner next to my bed. The place stinks and is poorly lit. What the fuck. Don't want to go back to it for awhile, at a restaurant now, waiting on the food, after I eat, I have to find something to do with the time. Probably go down to the train station and look at the bums, at least the light is better there.

These nights off are no good, without the confrontation and the noise, I turn on myself, I don't know where to go with the energy. I feel like punching the walls, or someone's face. I don't want to come back to the states, I feel more at home on the road here. I have been thinking a lot, riding in the back of the car, the more I think, the more inside myself I go, I don't talk much these days, it's a useless energy waste. Every time I go to one of these filthy cities, it's like wading thru a muddy river. These places move crooked and quick. Every night I play, I get stronger. Every time one of these people gets in my face and I deal on them, I get stronger. Everyday I stay out here, the farther away I get from their world. Makes me think of something Nietzsche said "He who was lost to the world now becomes free to conquer his own world." You want to hear all this? Of course not. Sometimes things come out. You know the last time I played this town they got me good. They burned me with cigars and cigarettes, I got punched in the mouth with the mic, real nice crowd. Fuck it, I'm still here. The weather reminds me of your corner of the world, it makes me remember last

February when you and I were walking around the square. It was good to see you this summer. I will send you something for your birthday, please send me your new address when you get it, I don't look forward to hearing about how your old roommates had a good howl over this letter. I will try to send this soon. Take good care of yourself, I think of you often. Don't let them destroy you.
Rollins out

. . .

I want her
Not a her
The her
The one that understands
War
The clanging heart
The storm
The obsession of a warrior
The blind painless addiction of glory
I open my eyes until they almost fall out
I turn my head from side to side
I cannot find her

. . .

Not human right now
I want to break things
If you were here, I would want you to touch me
Show me something, take me out of this thought
I am lost in my eyes
Touch me
Teach me a lesson that I forgot
I am high on war

. . .

In times like these I have to remember who I am
What I am
Where I come from
I come from war
My parents are war
I will survive

I will destroy
In times like these I think of three things
War
The number One
The forward roll
Deal with it
  . . .
You make me feel cold
When I talk to you I feel stupid and small
I tell you I miss you you say nothing
Frozen phone line
You tell me where it's at with your silence
I hang up the phone and look at the floor
The room is cold
One on none
That's the way it is
I get harder, I learn things
Things become clearer all the time
The idea of reaching out to someone else
Lodges in my throat and burns
I think about you tonight as I sit in this nowhere
Why are you like that to me
Why do I sit here and torture myself thinking about you
Long distance never felt longer
  . . .
I'm looking for something to scare me out of my skin
I'm following myself
Playing jokes on myself
Injecting myself with nightmares
I wait in dark corners to jump out and scare myself
I've got to get away from myself
  . . .
Cockroach blues
I don't want to fight you
I don't want to fuck you
I don't want anything from you

You want to exterminate me
I see you coming
You see me running
I know you
That's why I don't trust you
If you want to kill me
You better do it all the way
You're bigger stronger and smarter than I am
I know about being hated and hunted
It keeps me aware and strong
So like I said, you better do it all the way
You rip my guts out
Cut me in half
Break my legs
I keep crawling
You want to destroy me
It won't be as easy as you think
    . . .

Shit no, I don't want to go back there
Trips getting longer
The sun is setting in front of me
Sitting in a Dutch hotel room
All of a sudden the road pushes itself thru my face
I can't go back
Riding in the night car
Stars up in the sky for me
The only place I can think of is the next one.
Where ever that is
If I sit still I will fall apart
I will hear the calling sounds
Get filled with miles of empty box car dreams
Start finding more than nothing in the ghetto of a smile
I don't want to go back there
I think of the train I will ride this winter
Snow fields and black mirror windows
I am endless in my end

I am losing my grip on the heavy possession lie
I have myself
That's plenty
People make me lonely
Loneliness makes me want to move

. . .

If you want to do it
Then shut the fuck up and hit the road
If you want to see the real wheel roll
Then go out and roll it
Leave no note and move out
Otherwise you're just talking shit

. . .

I need discipline
More than most
I am hard on myself because of what I know
Without the discipline I would fall apart
I am not made of much

. . .

I am inside pulling in tight
Inner core getting harder
The number One growing in my brain
My eyes see clearly
My ears hear perfectly well
I've been thru the flesh mill
Carousel funeral march parade of lies
Tears and fake inspiration
They don't move me
I know what they say
Little words from little planets
Their lies don't cut me
Their touch doesn't make me feel
I am all the time
And just because they can't see it
Doesn't stop the truth bullet from ripping thru my brain
Work

Strength
Solitude
. . .

Familiarity breeds contempt I
You could see so much that you could go blind
You can think yourself stupid
Familiarity breeds contempt
Don't come near me
Don't call on me for anything
Don't knock on my door
I like you
Don't get close
I will eat you
I will turn you around
So you will see me for real
You will quickly hate
Quicker still
Turn away
Before we lose our fragile distance
. . .

Familiarity breeds contempt II
I wish you would touch me
It's been so long since any one touched me
I forget what it's like
Find me out
If I really liked you I would stay away from you
Familiarity breeds contempt
It's a truth that infuriates me
Keeps me here
. . .

I am the keeper of the inner war
All these people trying to shove their peace down my throat
Telling me to get in love's line
Sometimes it's hard to find war
I look around and all I see is peace
They would like me to trade my fangs for dentures

If they could they would make me crawl for peace
. . .
Desire locked itself in a room
Shot itself in the mouth
Couldn't get satisfaction any other way
. . .
I touch a shocking wire at the line
Each breath brings me closer
Don't send me a love letter
I don't need it
I am not hungry
I am not cold
I am not lonely
I am high on the end of the line
. . .
I am a hate fueled Hot Animal Machine
Hate feeds me
Keeps me warm
Makes me see clearly
My hate cuts thru lies
Just like he said:
There's nothing I detest more than the stench of lies
I am a hater
I am the one
I am the hate
Fuckers
I crush you with each breath
. . .
Yes I am negative to you
Yes I am all those things you called me
All the things your mamma called me too
I am all the things you can't get to
I am huge
I am invisible
. . .
Be careful

I am not given to emotion
Self possession is my thing
The feeding fist will be mine
I am the bullet
The casing
The charge
Like the bullet, I will go thru you
Or your fucking mom
If I become flattened
Destroyed
So what
    . . .
Reality's pitfalls...
Fuck you and your tape recorder face
There are no pitfalls in reality
The hole you drop down and disappear in
Is another one of your lies
So write a song or a little poem about it
    . . .
One of many truths
In all my life
I have never had an experience that came anywhere near
The level of awareness I have achieved
Thru an action of violence or aggression towards a human being
Breaking someone's nose is more memorable than the best sex
So many nights I crave a body to destroy
Sometimes I get it
    . . .
I am the only man street walker
I am the footstep sound moving past your window
I pass thru your dreams at night
When the cars pass me they send echoes thru my head
Street lamps glow
Reflections come up from the rain drenched sidewalk
I air out my brain at night
Lose an entire day of useless commotion

Do my best to get back to myself
Try to remember whatever it is

. . .

You're beautiful
Your body is perfect
You're 7 years younger than I am
You want me
You make me feel old and ugly
Shriveled and pale
Touching you made me feel like a fool
It was like a science project
That was months ago
Now I'm on a cold room thousands of miles away
Makes me feel shiftless
I want to ride a train into the night
Make the perfect getaway from myself
Thinking of you makes me want to get away from all humans
You make me see thru the frail human parade
The paper thin stability
The fragile human element
I want to disfigure my face
I want to move so fast that I become a blur
Everything about you makes me feel ugly

. . .

It's so close to me I don't want to say it out loud
It's wrapped up in the night wind
This thing that blows thru me
Sealed in a black envelope
The feeling I get when I am walking alone on an autumn night
The lightness
Ian might be able to tell you
So many thoughts wait for the night
Sometimes you get to be alive

. . .

12.6.87
Got off the plane 11 hours ago

Already it's getting to me
I re-live this over and over
The first evening back in the room
Everything is covered with dust and grime
Takes me all night to find half the stuff I'm looking for
I don't remember what's in this place anymore
Been gone 4-1/2 months
Been cleaning the room for hours now
Servicing it
The new old cell
I'm back

   . . .

I got a letter from a girl
Ten pages long
She's been off heroin two weeks now
She says she was on for 18 months
She says she loves me
She wants to die while fucking me
She hates life
She hates her parents
She tells me that we have met before
She is a model
I put the letter back in the envelope
A piece of paper falls out
Her portfolio
Pictures of her in bikinis
I remember her
There's a number on the paper
I call it
A woman at the other end says she's gone
Before she left, she forged a check for 250 dollars
I tell the woman about the letter
She says that the girl is messed up
Now I'm sitting in my room
Wagner pounding the walls
Sometimes people invade me

I read the letters they send me
It's as if they have moved into my brain
I hate the feeling of being crowded
When I'm alone in my room

   . . .

I was on the bus going east on Sunset
This guy gets on
He goes all the way to the back
His head goes from side to side
He looks at everyone coming like they're going to attack him
He looks frantic, like a caged animal
He keeps looking at me
I see a name tattooed on his neck
He has tattoos on his face
He comes over to me and asks me where I get my stuff done
I tell him about Rick
He tells me that he is covered
But has never gotten "a real one".
He says that his homeboys do his work for him
And now that he is "out"
He wants to get a lot of it covered up
He just finished 3 years straight time
Northern California
He was only supposed to be there for 18 months
But had to stay because of fighting
"The north and the south don't like each other,
  so there was a lot of rioting, I had to stay."
His nose is running and he keeps scratching his face
He says he can't get off heroin and coke
Today he is drinking beer to try to keep his mind off it
Yesterday he could barely stop himself from stealing a car
"I'm a dope fiend man"
The cigarette behind his ear falls behind the seat
Takes him two stops but he gets it back
He looks at me closely
"You're that guy, I see you in magazines that

my homeboys send me, you're that Rollins dude"
He went to his last two parole hearings fucked up
They found the dope in his urine
They will probably send him back for another year
He says it's ok
That's where all his friends are
He has been out four weeks now
He has a night job
He spends all the money on dope
He gets up to leave
He is off to meet his friend
They are going to try and score
"Hey homey, don't get no tattoos on your face
 no one understands"

 . . .

I tell you
He's in love with her and it's tearing him apart
The oldest and coldest story going since death
He loves her
She loves junk
She gets high
He gets lies
She drags him thru her methadone treatments
She always goes back to smack
To hold onto her
He started shooting too
That's what I call true love
He isn't hooked
He's just been checking it out for three months
She left him

 . . .

That last phone call was a good one
Hearing that girl lie her ass off
I like it when people lie so earnestly
Makes me know more about how you all work
She is all cleaned up

She sounds like a witch
Almost as funny as the call that came right before hers
The ex-boyfriend not knowing how much of an ex he is
Telling me how he is going to get back with her
He told me that she said
That she and I shoot up together
And it's alright by him
He has a few of my records
But don't share needles ok?
That's rich
You all are better than MTV
I ask her about the guy that she wasted and used back there
She starts laughing like she and I are in this together
She says that he got in over his head
And his mother is lucky she didn't make the check out for more
I guess mom is lucky
You make me hate

. . .

They are a disease
Something I never wanted
To stay strong I must stay away from them
I fuck myself up when I am around them
Every day I go without being touched
I get stronger
I see clearer
I can feel the precision
To want makes me feel alive
To feel so alone that I might disappear
Makes me want to live
Better than company
I want to build walls where there are none
So I can have something to break thru
The night passes so slow
The silence slices into me

. . .

It's the road I'm on

It takes me the long way
Around everything and everyone
I keep going, getting farther out
Sometimes I can't find things
Can't find words
Can't find a way
There's often a feeling of great loss
It's just the road I am on
Sometimes I get locked out of myself
It keeps me away from you
Even when I don't want to be
It hurts
If I knew what to say to you
I would scream it until you noticed
But when I look at you
No words come out
It's just the road I'm on
I never asked you to come along
I will never ask you
I like where I am
I wish I could like where you are
  . . .
I have been off the road for 3 days now
The sinking feeling is strong within me now
Some people called me today
I had nothing to say
I pulled the plug
It's better now
I have not touched a woman in 5 months
I think about what I would say to one if she was here right now
I can't think of anything
  . . .
This fever that I feel
Here alone in this room
I am untranslatable
Solitary refinement is keeping me together right now

A current runs thru me
Sometimes I expect to fly apart
Their existence drains me
This fever that I feel has no language outside myself
Trying to talk makes me feel so cold

. . .

Back in LA for awhile
At night I sit on the porch and look to the west
I can see the lights of Hollywood
Sunset Blvd. roaring like a diseased beast
This is the perfect place for the air strike
I was on Hollywood Blvd. tonight
Looking at the whores and punks and tourists
This place is dead already
Lying on its side, exhaling bad breath
I could clean it up
Call in the air strike
Do this place a favor, it should be incinerated
It's what happens when a city falls apart
The scum come out to hunt the scum
Leeches leeching leeches
The same tired black blood being passed
Mouth to mouth, needle to needle
Cleanse with fire
End this petty glittering palace of emptiness

. . .

Riding on the bus west on Santa Monica Blvd.
Nonstop ugly people
Some guy's dick in my face
The bus makes a turn, he leans into me
At Western Ave. more people get in than got out
The bus driver says to give your seat to a senior citizen
There's all these old folks hanging on for dear life
They look around to see if anyone is giving up a seat
No one moves
The bus driver repeats the request

All the seated look at the ground
We hit Beverly hills and everyone starts looking better
Except the sleeping drunk, breathing in my face
This fat guy in a security guard outfit is trying to talk to all the
people in the back. He's sitting next to me and he keeps trying to
catch my eye. I look straight ahead, I don't want to talk to this
asshole pig. He talks to the Mexican ladies in their maid uniforms,
they don't know any English and they try to be polite. They smile
and nod. The pig doesn't get it. The bus driver keeps slamming on
the brakes and I keep falling into him, we pitch and toss
A real ship of fools
I do my business and get on the bus and head east
Back to beautiful, pulsating, vibrant, now
Fabulous, cosmopolitan, metropolitan
Silverlake
Home of the stores that close at 8
And who cares anyway, the food on the shelves is stale
Why go outside at all
There's more aggravated assault than last year
Not one girl on the bus to look at
The side windows have been kicked out
Who cares, we're on a lark!
Pulling away from a stop a fist slams the glass where my head is
The bus pulls over and a man gets on
He's pissed off for almost getting left behind
Two old ladies get on
The driver pulls away fast
One of them falls and hits the floor hard
I guess the driver didn't see her white cane
Bad luck
A few stops later a group of homeboys get on
I can smell the wine and pot as they pass
I know I am getting close to my home
All the whites are getting off the bus
Two stops to go
I laugh out loud thinking about the guy

That walked out the back door right into a light pole
I did that when I was in 6th grade
I get out
63 minutes after Santa Monica
The stores are closed
The leather boys are out
Good night

. . .

Night time
Walking to the liquor store
Only thing that's open at this hour
I can see the lights of Hollywood
I can hear the sound of the freeway
Sounds like a war drawing to a close
Like an animal spitting out its last mouthful
Everything looks cool under the crime lights
The cars that pass me all sound like they are dying
Nothing runs well in this neighborhood
I do my business at the store
The Asian man never says a word to me
I walk out and pass the gay diner
All the faggots in the window check me out
So nice to be wanted
Two gay boys pass me
One says good evening and gives me the up and down
The other one laughs and they keep going
Under the crime lights nothing grows
Everything stays so it can die over and over
I get back to the room
I have found a new way to punish myself
All I have to do is go outside

. . .

I live in this room
I had to make it a good place to go
It's cold in this room
I had to make it warm in my brain

The bathroom stinks
It crawls into my nose
I smell it when I stand over the sink jerking off
I am alone in here
Some need others to make their place a good place to be
I think that would ruin it.
Out there is fucked up and filthy
Full of cheap weak nothings and nowheres
Not in here
What makes this place so good is the fact that in here
I don't have to explain shit to anyone
Too much time is taken up explaining
Trying to make yourself look good to someone else
That shit doesn't matter
It wastes your time
You don't owe anyone an explanation
When you get into that shit you end up lying at least once
That's a taste of cancer right there
I got so tired of it
I had to get off that bus
No one will ever understand you
They just won't
That's why my phone is unplugged tonight
That's why my door is locked tonight
That's why my gun is loaded tonight

    . . .

It's winter time
I'm in the same place I was last year
The winter brain
I crawl the walls
I wait for the hot nights
I've been here a week
My head is getting smashed on bullshit
I walk the perimeter of the room
I avoid human contact
They make me want to kill

I can't take the talk
After what I have been thru, I just can't take it
In my head it's summer
Incineration
Loud violent and real
I want to put my fist thru
I want to destroy
I have to maintain
The room gets so small at times like these
I don't talk to women
I don't like the way they make me feel
I want to wreck myself on something
War in the summer
I will fucking kill you
It all happens in the summer
I got it good last summer
I know what I am made of
Every night I shoved myself down my own throat
Some nights it hurt so bad I don't know how I got thru
I can't find anything that good anywhere else
This room is sucking life out of me
    . . .
Yea I'll go
Tonight?
Chicago?
Amtrak?
I'll go
Let's get the hell out of here
This is no place for the likes of us
As soon as we get there, we'll catch our breath
And then we'll get the hell out of there
I want to move now and forever
If I'm lucky
I'll get going so fast and go out like a shooting star
You will look up into the night sky
And say that you knew I would burn out sometime

. . .

You want to fuck me.
So what
You pat me on the dick like I'm a good dog
You want to fuck me but you don't want to know me
That makes me feel old and used
It took me awhile to figure it out
I remember now,
How you would get cold when I would try to talk to you.
Wanting nothing to do with me
Unless it was the right place and time.
That must have been a hardcore get off
To fuck without a thought as to who you're fucking
What a waste of time
Wanting you to be a human being
You're typical

. . .

I am a stranger passing you by
You couldn't look me in the eye if I was in your face right now
I don't want you to know me
I wish I didn't know you
I wish I didn't know everything about you
I am chased by your nightmares
You make me sick
I wish you weren't so common
So see-thru
So weak and dangerous
In such great abundance
I am the stranger
The night train
The feeling at the back of your neck
I had to die many times
I had to rip your tubes out of my arm
I had to open my eyes all the way
I had to rip the lids off so they couldn't close
I had to spend years spitting out the poison

All the love
You will never filthify my existence again
Every day I work hard to untangle myself from your world
I can't get far enough away

  .   .   .

I asked her if we could we go out sometime
She said there was no point
We had nothing in common
We did anyway
Weeks later I found out that she was right
Maybe I am evolving into a different species

  .   .   .

I come home to see how the roommate has cared for the house
She is a living shit bag
A triumph for decadence
This place is covered with dirt
Looks like a bunch of fucking pigs have been living here
I hate it when the weak get a chance
To bring everything down to their level
There's roaches crawling all over the place
What a drag to have to live here
Cat shit smell
Everything covered with ashes and cat hair
Low self esteem
They treat everything like they treat themselves
Like shit
Someday I'll move out of this shit hole

  .   .   .

Last night I was in the kitchen
This roach runs by me heading for the stove
I nailed it with my index finger, knocked part of its guts out
The roach kept crawling, dragging its guts behind
I pushed it back so it couldn't get away
The rear legs gave out, it kept crawling
The guts started to pick up dirt and bits of food
It still kept going with all the new weight

I wondered if I would be able to keep on crawling
With my guts hanging out of me like that
I would have done something lame
like gone into shock and died
Finally I killed it
Tonight I was at the market
I got my food and was walking towards the door
There was a small line to get out
A woman with a walker was having trouble getting out
People were bumping into her, getting around her
They couldn't wait that long
She nearly got knocked over a few times
Still she kept on crawling
She had a hunched back
She edged up to a trash can
I saw her bend over it
I wondered if she was looking for food
I got closer and saw that she was crying
Her tears were falling into the trashcan
Tears out with the garbage
I could hear her crying
Crying into a trash can as people pushed by her
At some point, every living thing is made to crawl
They'll always make you crawl if they can
She looked so lost there under the Christmas lights
. . .

I'll kill the fuckers. They better not come near me, I'll kill them, do
you hear me? I'll rip their fucking pig eyes out, they don't know
what they're dealing with here. Don't push me, I know that you're
out to get me, you think that I don't know that? You came to the
wrong place, I'm gonna turn your world into a pile of shit.
I don't want to be here
Oh lord should I shoot myself tonight
I want to be loved
There's no one here who loves me
I want to be touched

Nobody better touch me
Should I hang myself tonight
I want to skin myself alive
But I'm too afraid to try
I want to stick my tongue in a live wire socket
I'm spinning
I hate
I hate my life
It's a dirty stranger
Life molests me
Long greasy fingers
I do it to myself
Should I kill myself tonight
They want to smash my head. Did you hear me, they want to smash
my brains out onto my shoes. I know what they say about me, I
know what you say about me too. You think that I don't know
anything, that's why you think you can get away with all the crime
that you do. They inject me with nightmares, special dreams to
make me crazy, they want to fill me with their fear. They don't
know that I get stronger off their fear, one day I'm going to give it
all back to them and then they'll all be sorry they ever messed with
me.
Oh lord I think I hear angels singing
Maybe it's just the water in the pipes
Should I jump off the roof tonight
My dreams are sweating
They burst into flames in front of my eyes
Everything in this room is alive except me
They killed me
All the knives and needles in my eyes.
Do you know how it feels when it all falls away
You start shaking
You lose your grip
Fragile and vicious
Lashing out with the razors of self hatred
1000 eyes sprout out of your head

You see too much
It drives you insane
Get out from under the floor boards you sons of bitches, I hear you
under there, trying to spy, trying to listen into my thoughts. You
spend your whole life trying to make me kill myself. That's all you
can do, you got nothing. I'll take you to hell and keep you there for
awhile. You can't live inside me anymore. I have my own mind...
. . .
They invade me with their calls
Months ago she called me
Told me that the medication was making her overweight
Now no longer on the medication
Nor depressed or overweight
The last time she called was in the middle of the night
She wouldn't stop talking, said she was falling apart
This time she is in love
She asks me what I'm doing
I tell her that I am working
I don't want to talk about it, I just want to do it
They spend so much time talking about it
They talk themselves in and out of insane asylums
Talk talk talk
Like they have all the time in the world
Like they have all of my time as well
I felt like throwing the phone across the room
Finally she released me
I had my room to myself again
. . .
We could get away from here
Give them all the slip
It wouldn't last long
You would be surprised how fast they find you
I was just thinking of you
You who I've never seen
I don't know if you exist
Perhaps we will find each other in this mess

Do you ever feel closed in?
Like you could walk for miles and go nowhere?
Do you feel the distance when you're close to someone?
When you see the truth and wish you didn't
I can't get away from the truth
The sands of the hourglass are the scars that I bear
Is there somewhere we could go?
A house that's burning?
A place that's like you and me
Temporary
. . .

Sitting in the room, I should be gone
There's nothing left but the road
I laugh at the lines in my face
Tell me about your broken dreams
About your broken television set
About your fear
We take up all of our time
We waste a life thinking that we have to live correctly
It makes us shrink back from the sun, retire to the shadows
There are some that walk away from the world
They are the ones that get written about
We make a few into heroes so we can live thru them
Some of them are stupid enough to wait around for the praise
They lose the sound that roars in their ears
They forget the feeling of the pain
It's sad to see them go out like they do
Best not to talk about it
Best to go on and head for the jungle
When you go, if you ever do
Do it right
Head out for the darkest part
. . .

A few weeks ago, I was in Germany
Did this show in Munich
I could feel my guts falling thru my shoes as I spoke

After it was over
People were coming up to me, shaking my hand, hugging me
The nicer they were, the deeper I sank
These girls were waiting to meet me
I didn't want to mess with it
I got out of there
I remember the rest of the night in the hotel room
I carry it like a hunch back
Night by night, I freeze out parts of myself
What is there after it's all gone
Truth, I'm coming

. . .

Have you seen the down men
The ones who live in the cold shadows
Broken knuckles
The ones with tears behind their eyes
The only ones
Leftovers from the last two wars
Dislocated, left to fade away
Shuffling along the crust of civilization
They have forgotten themselves for the better
For them, it's all down time

. . .

I am the human unraveling thing
I peel layers and cast them off like some kind of animal act
It's ugly
The human navel orange
I like things that are ugly
They tell me everything
An addiction to truth will leave you in a pile on the floor
Make you sick of yourself
Rip yourself apart
Walk until it falls away
Seek darkness until you see blinding light
Know that there are too many cowards in the world
They speak the loudest

. . .

I am waiting for the burning rain
I am waiting for the fire to rip right thru me
I am the endless walking thing
I am the terminal
The termination
It all pulls together
Turns my vision into cataract tissue

. . .

I pulled myself away from them
I needed to find myself
It's easy to get lost, too easy, too painless
I want to know when I am bleeding to death
Walked out of the room of sporadic sexual encounters
Didn't feel good
Life burns and freezes me
A lot of times it leaves me alone
Taunts me
Makes me think that I will break
So let it break, I want to see the pieces
At least I'll know something
I need to know something
Even if it kills me

. . .

Post Lhasa Club Blues
Did a show about two hours ago
Was up there spilling my guts for a long time
All these people were there, and all the lights were on
It felt good
Now I'm in my room alone
3:30 in the morning
It's the emptiness that makes it hard to sleep
When you can't take your mind off your mind
Maybe it's not good to feel that good
The other side of it is too much sometimes
Like right now

. . .

Don't let them look at you for too long
They will make you the axis for their woes
If you're not careful their problems will become yours
And if you can't take the weight
They'll call you every name in the book
They have a way of calling revenge self-affirmation
And they will affirm themselves on your flesh all night long
Watch out for the weak

. . .

I'm ok but my heart is stupid
It goes places that I would never go
I have a leash that I keep it on
Doesn't always work
Never learns from pain
Stupid

. . .

No Friends In This City:
I like you so I'll tell you straight
Don't try to get close to me
No one does
When they think they are
They hurt themselves and they don't feel it
I don't want you to hurt yourself
If you try to get close to me you turn yourself into shit
The best thing for you to do is to walk out of this place
If it's a game you're playing, you will lose
You don't want to be a loser in a place like this
Just because we fuck, doesn't mean anything more
Than that we fuck
I'm not someone who cares about you
You haven't ripped me off yet, so I like you alright
I'm telling you, the best thing to do is to get out of here
I will make everything turn on you
It's all I know how to do
I will laugh in your face and you will cry

You have no friends in this city
No one does
I am the glittering saint of hollowness
You see how I shine
You see the other fools lined up behind you
Just because you're at the front of the line
Doesn't mean that you're not in line
Do you see what I mean?
Walk away before you crawl

   . . .

I am weak
Looking to get stronger
When I open my eyes all the way
It's all there is for me
Kindness is strength
It's easier to close a door, than to keep it open
Hatred is easy
Frustration is life on pause
These are truths that are hard for me to deal with
I learned a lot this year
I think I am stronger than last year
Self creation is painful
Trying to take my parent's blood out of mine
Trying to stand on my own two feet
Without leaning on someone else
Looking to myself for total strength
To be
One
From
None

Robert Fischer: You have two allies: discipline and insanity.

ROLLINS: Yep. Gets me through the hard times.

RF: Is the one the consequence of the other ?

ROLLINS: For me, discipline is a survival mode, a survival mechanism. Insanity is another. Insanity gives me a chance to see things in a different way, it's a temporary state. Discipline is an all-the-time thing for me, it has to be. Discipline is important to me. That's the way I was raised, it's what I know and it's what I understand.

RF: So, discipline is not to keep off insanity.

ROLLINS: I think the two go hand in hand.

RF: You take advantage of insanity?

ROLLINS: Insanity enters into a lot of what I do because I work myself into extreme states of mind, it's just the nature of what I do. And to beat the come-down of all that, for me, to do this takes great amounts of discipline. To keep from going off the deep end a lot of times, if you can believe that. It's hard to maintain. Especially when I am not in a situation where I can release tension. That's why I like to do shows all the time. It's a good way to get what's inside of me out, if I don't get what's inside of me out, it bottles up and it turns on me, I do stupid things to myself and others.

RF: But that's not insanity. This doesn't turn up as insanity. It's not "that insanity" you are talking about.

ROLLINS: The pitches of insanity I reach are from dealing with what is in front of me on a day to day basis. It's hard for me to contain and maintain myself in a normal sense, perhaps it's because of the way I am, I don't know. I know that I relate to people and situations differently than a lot people I've met.

RF: But what was first in your life, discipline or insanity?

ROLLINS: Discipline.

RF: So, insanity has to do with maintaining control and losing control? The mechanisms of control and ultimately with the system that wants you to be "sane", so insanity would be a way of escaping or dealing with or destroying the structures of the system.

ROLLINS: A system that potentially confines me, oppresses me: insanity is one way of dealing with it. Not a cop-out though, I think that most people's reality is completely insane. I consider a lot people insane. So, in the straight world context, I am insane. I couldn't do what a lot of people do with themselves. I don't think like that. That's not the way I am. It takes many hardships to be different, because you stick out and you have to deal with it, that's what I keep coming back to, I keep turning to, having to deal with that.

RF: But normality, or so-called normality.

ROLLINS: Which to me, along with insanity, is a very relative term.

RF: The so-called normality actually keeps people from being themselves.

ROLLINS: Yes.

RF: So, actually being insane is being free.

ROLLINS: Yes, because sanity and normality has a whole lot to do with oppression, repression, denial. Denial of what you really feel.

RF: False values.

ROLLINS: Living lies, I'm not interested in that.

RF: And not being yourself.

ROLLINS: Yes, living someone else's trip. No thanks.

RF: In this society everything is geared to put you back to normality, even if they have an increasingly hard time because their so-called sanity is falling to pieces.

ROLLINS: A lot of people shirk reality, avoid reality. Reality is a river with a fierce current, you can try to resist it but the current never stops. It will go longer and harder than you ever will. All these people go against the way of reality and eventually get tired, society gets tired, cities get tired, ways of life get tired, civilization gets tired, language gets tired, finally it goes the way of the river. It goes the way of the real flow, and you can see it now, you can see it all over the place. That's why the shit is breaking down. That's why you're getting more diseases, that's why you're getting more murder and rape, jails overflowing because you can't shirk reality, the more you deny it, the more cancerous you get. I choose not to back off. People say: Hey, how come you're so negative. I am not negative. You're negative! How can you say I'm negative when I opt to deal with it. To deal with myself and not to be afraid to say that I feel this way about this. People are so uptight, the only things that can save them make them uptight: Themselves. They lie. I'm nothing much, I am not brilliant, but even an average mind like mine can take a look around and see what's happening. It doesn't take any kind of genius to see the shit is disintegrating around you. People in the future will have to be very disciplined. Youth must be disciplined. I regret that I was not raised with more discipline. I wish now that I had been sent to a military academy. I mean it, all the discipline I was raised on in school helps me a lot now. My father was a very disciplined man. The school I went to for seven years was a disciplinary school. Discipline has got me through hard times, not love and not my brain. I've been able to hang in there and not lose it. I keep moving. It takes discipline for me to do that. Maybe it's easier for others to do it another way. I have to work harder and longer to get done the work others do in next to no time. I'm not good at what I do, that's why I need discipline to keep it rolling.

RF: But then, you can be disciplined with the things of this creation. You could say: try to have respect for your belongings, and for the objects of this earth. Don't litter. So, on the one side there is a material oriented way of discipline which is mechanical.

ROLLINS: Sure, but that has roots, this kind of discipline: don't steal, don't destroy the planet. To me, this is all very well and good, right on. This is having respect for material value. I think having self-respect is more important. Someone who has self-respect is strong. Even if a guy weighs 135 Pounds and can't pick up his suitcase, if he respects himself, he is as strong as some one who could throw him across the street, maybe stronger. Anyone with real self-respect wouldn't litter, wouldn't steal, wouldn't lie, wouldn't fuck anyone else over. He wouldn't do anything to anyone else that he wouldn't do to himself. When I respect myself, I don't need to take out my pain or weakness out on someone else. You hate yourself and you'll hate everything around you, it's easy to get lost in yourself.

RF: Then discipline and insanity can be considered as the two faces of one coin, discipline being more concerned with outer values and insanity with moral and spiritual values.

ROLLINS: That sounds good.

RF: You tour a lot and you're mostly in situations in which you constantly have to cope with people coming for autographs, for interviews, hustling you all the time, wanting to touch you. You don't have much privacy. And there's the particular situation when you are touring Europe, where you don't know the language. Do you feel any alienation?

ROLLINS: Yes and no. Ok, I prefer being in countries where they don't speak English. I came to this conclusion after living for months in Europe. I had been here since early August, in continental Europe for 13 weeks straight. Then I had to go to England. I get to the ferry dock and there's all these people waiting to go on the boat, people from the UK, It was the first time I heard English spoken all around me for 13 weeks. It was strange because suddenly I'm listening to all these mundane conversations about things in which I have no interest. Since I know the language, I have no choice but to understand it, I can't shut them out. So, I was thinking of how much time I waste, how much time is taken from me, by word-pollution, by being strung along. By not understanding someone's language, I avoid that. Even billboards, magazines, and advertisements I saw in Germany for example, I couldn't understand much about them. After a while I stopped looking, stopped acknowledging them. When I got to England, I could read everything and once more I was having all this stuff laid on me. I can't help it, I look around and I can read everything that's in English whether I want to or not, I see it and it has already assaulted me. And so, in that way I am not bothered with that kind of situation in Europe because I have a lot more time for myself and a lot more thinking can be done. I can concentrate a lot more. It took me a while to be able to get to that point. At first, when I would be sitting around with a bunch of people who were talking in their native language, it was very distracting, now I have it turned out to the level where it's just noise and I can have silence all around me. But as far as feeling alien, as opposed to feeling familiar, no, because I came to the conclusion that I don't want "in". I don't feel that I'm missing out on something. I am not on the outside looking in. I'm on the outside looking out. I've got my back turned to them.

RF: Some of the conclusions you are writing down day by day mention this kind of thing.

ROLLINS: I found a new home. I moved in a room much better than in England. I moved into a better neighborhood. I moved into my head. That's my planet, that's my neighborhood, I'm at the point where I can sit in a room alone and be perfectly content in my own company.

RF: You feel at ease with alienation.

ROLLINS: Yes. I like alienation, it's a cool ride, you know. At least you know where you're at. When people come up to you, shaking your hand and smiling at you, wanting to give you things and wanting to be your friend, you don't always know where you're at. You always know where you're at with your enemies. And when you're on the outside you always know where you are.

RF: This functions also in the States.

ROLLINS: It doesn't matter where I am.

RF: And then comes up the thing with reality. When people are coming up to you and treating you like a celebrity, like a star, which is a completely artificial construct, it makes you understand that none of it is real, or is it that "Maybe I am the one that is not real", like you say in one of your books, "Maybe I am the one who has it all screwed up in my brain". So what is real?

ROLLINS: For me what is real is the intent that is in your heart. Ok, when all these people come up to me and they want my autograph, I do it for them, I don't say: "Go away !". I'm not like that. What I try to do is to make some kind of human contact with the person so that they can see the truth, which is that I am there like they are there and it's no big deal, we can see eye to eye, that there doesn't have to be some kind of star trip going on.

RF: On stage, you play out, on stage, you are super-real, you somehow extrapolate your own role, making it bigger so as to catalyze some energies.

ROLLINS: I know about energy. I can take everybody's energy but I give it back. I have to feel all those things, and that violence, that speed and that intensity, physically and mentally and spiritually it changes me. Those changes are permanent. I cannot undo what I have done to myself. What I do makes me what I am, it defines me. If I stop today, I will still be that way. What I have done to myself is irreversible. The present reality in which I exist in, is the most real place I've ever been, it's undeniable, you know. I can't deny it, I can't fight it. I can't disagree with the truth.

RF: And isn't that insanity.

ROLLINS: Yes. My reality could be someone else's insanity, and when I get a chance to look at myself, whoa!

RF: Do you ever get touched by the temptation of cynicism?

ROLLINS: Cynicism, I have to fight it very hard. I think that there's a fine line between cynicism and a good, healthy attitude of questioning things. To me, a lot of cynics are reactionary. They always say: "I know that". And they don't even check it out. In the mind of the cynic, everything that you've been doing is "old", "been done", "ridiculous", "pointless", and they don't even know your name. A lot of times, they don't even check out the things that they say that they're against. Perhaps they're burnt out and don't want anyone to know. I think a lot of cynicism comes from just that, the fact that it's easier to put labels on things and to say something sucks rather than going and checking it out, hell I've done that enough times!

RF: Cynicism has also to do with a false way of emancipation.

ROLLINS: I don't know what emancipation means.

RF: People think that they have understood something.

ROLLINS: It's true that a lot of cynical people pretend that they have an understanding of certain things, that's why they feel this way. But the funny thing is that cynics often get their information from outside their own headquarters. They get their information, their attitude from a magazine, from television, from things based and built from the ground up on bullshit. So it's taking bullshit and molding it into a castle and molding it into a shape of your own. It's just not your own idea. That's why I question a cynical mind.

RF: Cynicism is used ultimately to protect oneself from the bullshit. And today it has been reversed and exteriorized.

ROLLINS: I agree, but do you know who or what you're protecting yourself from? You're not always protecting yourself from the bullshit, you're protecting yourself from yourself. Ok, you became unaware of yourself and you think in a certain way about a certain thing. Without letting that thing come into you and letting it run through the different channels of yourself, you give it one single access channel. You deal the same way with totally different things and then you classify them. You have an apple next to a cow and you call them both rocks. Because of the bullshit that you've been fed. I question that a lot of times, because I ask: Is that your opinion, or is that an opinion you got from some place that you don't even remember? To me, that's why there's a difference between someone who is cynical and someone who questions things, and pursues an answer. He checks things out and gives them a chance to be accepted by their own merit. To me, cynicism is an extremely burned out way of gathering and processing information. I am not interested in cynicism, it crawls up its ass quickly.

RF: Sometimes it's a sign of desperation. I mean, the original cynics were these Greek philosophers who were living in a barrel, very poor. And when Alexander the Great came and said "So, you are the famous Diogenes, the cynical philosopher. You can ask me a favor and I will fulfill it." Diogenes said: "Get out of my sun." Which is a very desperate philosophy. That was the true meaning of cynicism. Nowadays, this desperation has turned wrong. It's fighting off a lie, which is ok, with another lie, which is wrong.

ROLLINS: Right. That's what I mean. That says it very well. I mean, they use information processed by bullshit and call it their truth, and it's based on total shit. A lot of people have opinions they got from television, they come and say that they saw it on TV so it must be true. They weren't there but they still have an opinion on it like they were, and they also pass a judgement based on assumption. I think that this leads to closed mindedness, that has always proven to be dangerous in my experience. I think that a closed mind is a desperate mind. And desperation gives way to panic, weakness, weakness is evil. Weakness is the only sin to me. It takes guts to check things out, it takes guts to take a stand and say "Wait a minute, I don't like this." Or "I like this." How many people won't like something because of what they read about it. They are not going to investigate. They're going to sit back and tell you what they heard on the evening news.

RF: This brings us back to the problem of reality, what is real? Nowadays truth IS what is said on TV. If they say on TV that shit is good and tastes like vanilla, and most of the time it's some Hollywood actor who tells them they'll eat it. This summer I have been watching the Iran-gate hearings, the Contra-Hearings on TV. For 3 weeks they tried to put together all these lies, and lots of people know that there is corruption, bribery and all this Mafiosi thing going on, and that's it's all going the wrong way. But on TV they put up a nice story that makes it look good. What is being said on TV winds up more real than what is happening in real life.

ROLLINS: A lot of people don't have time. They have to get to work. If they want to get out and check out something they'll be late, they'll lose their apartment. The Man has got you coming and going. You're not allowed to find your own opinion. The man can kick you out of your apartment. You don't want to get kicked out of your apartment. So you come home, nice and tired, turn on the 7 o'clock news and get your opinion and they'll sell you some beers in between, beers and cigarettes and stuff you can further dull and poison yourself with.

RF: Gives a meaning to your life.

ROLLINS: Sure, Their meaning! It keeps you working, it keeps you standing in line, it keeps you tired and it keeps you hanging on while they plug you into their fire breathing, man eating, life-support system and let you bleed to death, slowly. A good consumer.

RF: It appears to me, and maybe this is another aspect of your insanity: you are somehow addicted to this fighting.

ROLLINS: Sure. But as far as saying that my life is empty, sometimes I feel like that. But maybe it's because I do so much stuff. It's a case of "Can't see the forest because for the trees", you know. Sometimes, there's so much going on around me, I can't see the big picture.

RF: But then you feel emotional about it?

ROLLINS: Sometimes, but I don't relate the same way to people and things the way I used to.

RF: And then you want to go back on tour!

ROLLINS: Yes, yes. Sometimes that's the only thing I can do that makes sense. When I come home from tour it's like going off a train that's going a 100 miles an hour and you get off and you are still going a 100 miles an hour and everything around you is moving slow. When I come home from tours I go into very heavy depressions. Very bad depressions, like you get set up for this big long haul and you do it and at the finish line there's nothing. Glory has a hollow ring. It's a train that leaves you, in the morning you wake up and you're not the King of the Jungle, you're not on tour out there, you know, lean and mean and fierce. You're back in this watered-down, dull padded cell with all the lies that go with it. It's hard for me to maintain myself on that level. I get a lot less work done, I reach a point where I can't maintain my work load when I'm home. Because I realize now what I must do to be able to keep doing what I want to do. I am writing it down. I am doing a list right now of what I call the "Iron reminders" to keep myself from slipping.

I have to work very hard to maintain myself. These nice nights, you know, pleasant views, you know, then I drink some coffee, sit at my typewriter, and then I drink two cups of coffee and then I want to take a 45 minute shower and then I want to get down with some girl and then I start thinking about that girl a lot and I spend a lot of time just lying around fucking when I should be getting down the road. And then little things become big things. They don't stay little. Like: Oh, the girl doesn't want to talk to me me, which should be met with an "Ok". It goes from that to "What should I say, what did I do? Did I do something wrong? Should I call her, how come she hasn't called me?" Bullshit, bullshit. If I catch myself doing that, I go: Whoa, time to go on the road, time to get out of here, time to get back to work. Getting caught in the evil killing machine, getting caught up in the slow-down machine, in the no-mind machine. Just getting caught up in the stupid machine, I'm not interested in that. You can waste your whole fucking life doing that. Ok, to some people it's not a waste. Those who would rather sit around, moan about some relationship, if that's what they want to do? Ok, go ahead. You won't see me coming to their house trying to convince them otherwise. I've got no words of advice for anyone. If someone wants to go ahead with that time wasting masochistic torture they see fit to inflict upon themselves, fine. I've got my own torture I do to myself. Everyone's got their own way of whipping themselves. I've got mine. But some guy with his girlfriend, some girl with her boyfriend, that takes up all of their time that's their way of doing it. I know myself. The last time I was back in LA when the tour was over. I didn't want to go outside, I didn't leave the house for three days. I couldn't handle it. If someone looked at me, I wanted to rip their heads off. Riding on a bus, I couldn't handle riding on a bus. Some dude looking at my tattoos and making a face, I wanted to rip his face off and put it in his pocket. Or dealing with some girl, you know, I just couldn't. Imagine some guy coming home from Vietnam. One day he's in the jungle. Next day he's at the back. The day after, he flies to Japan. Takes day off to rest. He gets checked out. Days after being in the jungle, he is now driving his wife's car to the store. He makes a turn without using his signal, he gets pulled over by a cop. A fat cop who proceeds to give him a big bag of shit for not using a blinker. A week ago people were blowing up next to him and he was killing people. He was the law, now he's got some watered-down, fat asshole slapping his wrist because he didn't put on a blinker. You wonder why the Vet comes out of the car and beats the shit out of the cop and gets arrested? That's how I feel when I come home. That's how I feel when I have to deal with the luke-warm, soggy, weak realities of people when I come home. That's how I feel. I never been in war, except my own. I never went to Vietnam, I was too young. I would have gone.

RF: Because of the intensity?

ROLLINS: I would have been better off there.

RF: It somehow astonishes me that you put the blame, and I have heard it now a few times. You put the blame on stupid people. We know that people are stupid. But it is not all their fault. There is a purpose behind that. If you say, that the American Indians have become completely degenerated, you cannot say it is really their fault. On one side it is their own fault, of course. They could have been resisting the pressure. But their frame of mind was not made to cope with the Western mind who is out to conquer, to dominate, to control. I think it is the Western mind, the Western mind is a disease!

ROLLINS: I agree, Western society is a disease. Where I live, America that's all I really know, is a disease. It's raised on shit. It doesn't make a great deal of sense.

RF: And these people, living in the western society, are sick.

ROLLINS: In a way they are, racism, a lifestyle of convenience and apathy. That's what I would call sick. You see what I do. I don't go in the main stream and try to go upstream. I don't fight that kind. You won't see me standing there trying to convince anyone. I am not there to come down on people. I go out on tour. I find the place where I feel most comfortable. I don't feel comfortable in the main stream. I don't feel comfortable in the straight society. So you won't see me there, living in it, complaining about it, I left, I'm gone. I am where I want to be, I like what I do, I live on the road. I challenge myself in front of constantly changing variables.

RF: So you would say that the best way to contribute to change the world is to work on yourself.

ROLLINS: Sure. It's a good way, the more you know about yourself, certainly the less harm you're going to do to other people. And the way things go where I come from, people die and you don't know about it. A lot of people suffer for luxury where I come from. You go to Beverly Hills, you know, and those people just cashing out, but if you could see the blood and the broken hands of the Mexicans used in building those mansions, you would see a different thing. And the fact that you can get off ten exits down the highway and risk having your head blown off gives you an idea about the absurdity and the horror of the whole thing, it sucks to think about it.

RF: Yeah well, but at the same time, even these people in Beverly Hills, they suffer from this disease too, they too are victims.

ROLLINS: Ok, so stop being a victim. Stop putting your pain on someone else's flesh, and fight it yourself, by being yourself. If you are someone else and you opt for someone else's dream and don't get on your own you probably destroy someone next to you. If some man has a cocaine habit and if he's got two kids at home, he's putting his shit on someone else's stick. When dad comes down from his cocaine binge and he's in a nasty mood it's the kids that get whacked. His victimization of his kids and wife is the weak beating the handcuffed. It's these people drowning each other, all the hustle and bustle. Someone pulling down someone else by his leg and sitting on someone else's shoulders, and the guy, well this is his job: to have someone else sit on his shoulders.

RF: We are coming to the question of religion now, it seems to me that you choose the way of salvation through the bottom.

ROLLINS: Get down to rise, to paraphrase Nietzsche from Thus Spoke Zarathustra: I love he who comes from under. You have to go all the way to find your character.

RF: Did you have a religious education ?

ROLLINS: No. I never went to church. Nietzsche said a great thing about heaven and hell, about how it was an idea created by those who couldn't handle earth, who couldn't handle the pleasures of life. Thinking about it more, it's a good way to impose morality and law and instill fear and obedience. The thing that always put me off religion was the promise of punishment and eternal damnation for wanting to fuck and live freely. That someone would dare try to intimidate me with some fucking book and a story about angels and people walking on water and all this Walt Disney shit, adults! I guess some people, probably men, looking for a way to control those women! They can't deal with terra firma, so they make some kind of never-never land. It's so full of shit. I am not going to live in fear, I am not insecure. I don't buy into the idea of punishment and reward. There is no reward. There's no heaven that's to keep people going to work. Religion is based on fear, fear of death, fear of the unknown, fear of loneliness and social non acceptance. Fear and power. They utilize your fear to get power, but it's not power, not true power, it's force. Force is the weak man's version of power.

RF: What is there to be afraid of?

ROLLINS: Fearlessness. To me there's different levels of fear. On some levels I like fear, I believe in fear. Actually, with fear comes awareness if you choose to confront it. Fear can be the most powerful instrument of control and manipulation. And it is not courage that you need to confront fear with. With courage comes blindness. Say you have this guy, "Well Johnny, you're going to run out into that field with the enemy firing at you from holes in the ground", and he says: "I don't want to die". But: "Come on, Johnny. Where is your courage?" Ok: The guy runs out and gets destroyed. I think that "real guts" and all that, is for the most part, bullshit. But knowing your fear and the consequences and still trying to pull it off, being aware of what's going down, and dealing with it, in a calculated manner, that's a very different matter.

RF: And in your eyes, does fear have anything to do with insanity? The fear of not having any safeguards anymore for example.

ROLLINS: Reality is my safeguard, all things that are true, they are my safeguards.

RF: Insanity never makes you afraid ?

ROLLINS: No. I am always too busy being there. Though I have done some pretty far out shit. Stuff that when I later realized what I was doing, when I looked back at it a few days later, I couldn't believe I did something that stupid.

RF: You feel very strongly about Hubert Selby Jr. How did you get to meet him?

ROLLINS: For years people had been telling me about this book "Last Exit to Brooklyn" by Hubert Selby, I never heard of him, but I found a used copy and bought it and read it and was knocked out by the power of his writing. Soon after at a show I was doing, a man named Mike Griffin gave me a copy of Selby's third novel "The Demon". Mike said that this book was incredible and that I should read it now. I read it on an airplane going to Washington DC, I thought that the plane would crash from the hell coming out of that book. I thought he must have been following me, I saw so much of myself in his story, just the fuckedness and the obsession with bullshit. I asked others who had read that and I got the same reaction, Selby had read them like the Sunday papers. After a lot of looking and no success in finding his other titles "Requiem for a Dream" and "The Room", Mike lent them to me. After reading them, a depression settled over me. On finishing "Requiem", I found myself unable to write. His book was too good, I was intimidated and lost. I figured that I should just mow his lawn or something. Days later I found his number and called him and asked him if I could meet with him and get my book signed. He gave me his address and I went over there and we hung out for awhile. I gave him a couple of the books that I had done. I went home feeling stupid for being so moved by his work and I was pissed off for having allowed something to prevent me from working. Maybe I shouldn't have done it, maybe it's better not to meet people that I admire.

Five days later I get this phone call and it's Selby and he says: "Hey Rollins, I've been reading your book...". And I think, yeah well he'll just say thanks for the book and hang up, you know. But he says: "Goddamn, there's this line on page 19, fucking great!" You know, he read me my own book over the phone. And he says: "You're a fucking great writer". Wow, thanks! I was up probably half the night writing, that gave me such a jolt, that he liked my work. We became friends. He came to a couple of my shows and he really enjoyed himself and we started hanging out, eating, listening to music. He writes me letters and I write him letters. I have some of his letters with me and they're amazing. Powerful. He's my hero. I think he is the greatest living American author. That's my opinion. The guy has had a big impact on my life and, on my writing and he's one of those people in my life who made me go around a corner.

RF: When was that?

ROLLINS: That was about a year and a half ago. I refuse to allow him to go down into history unnoticed. If I had more money and more time and more knowledge, I would get all of his out of print titles in print, in America right now and get him where he should be, on the front shelf of every bookstore in the country. The guy wrote these books in the 70's and now, time has finally caught up with him. Now, people who didn't get it when it came out should be allowed to get it this time. I feel very strongly about that. I feel more strongly about his work than I do about mine.

RF: Selby has a cult-following but has never made it big.

ROLLINS: In many ways, the man got passed over, what he has to say is not pretty, and it isn't easy to take, it's real and it makes you see yourself and those around you and it's not easy to take it. We have been poisoned on so much shit for so many years, when the truth comes along and it's right in your face, you don't know what to do with it so you put it in the dark corner and leave it alone. One of the great things about his work is that it never leaves you alone, it sticks to you like paint, like napalm. To me, his work is good medicine. An interesting thing is, if you look at his paperbacks, if you can find one, for example "The Demon", they put a half naked woman on it, you know, the typical pulp-cover, woman with bra strap half-down, man with a drink in his hand, this urban contemporary thing. You look at the cover and see what this company is trying to sell. This is going nowhere. Anybody who opens the book is just locked in hell.

He works this boring straight job to pay his rent, and he's one of the ten mightiest authors in the last one hundred years to come out of America without a doubt. I asked him some time ago what he books he reads, I wanted to check out anybody who is on his reading list. He says to check out William Kennedy. He is well known in America. His last book won a Pulitzer Prize. The guy wrote these books about what's going on in New York, about the goings-on of the Mafia. His last book is called "Iron Weed". There's a movie coming out with Jack Nicholson and Faye Dunaway. The book is big, so I am reading this stuff that won the Pulitzer Prize and it doesn't hold a candle to Selby. It doesn't even touch him. I am not a big literati. I don't know a whole lot about books and I am not smart but, I never read anything that burned a hole right through me like Selby. Nothing. Not Celine, not Rimbaud, not Henry Miller, nothing. Nothing is scorching like Selby. Vonnegut, Mark Twain, Dostoievski, Nietzsche, maybe Nietzsche. This is just my opinion, you know. I am sure there's millions who disagree. Fine. But I am just wanting to make sure to do my part to be sure that the guy goes down into American history.

RF: How does he live ?

ROLLINS: A comfortable but small apartment. He is a modest man. After all the shit he's been through, the fact that he is still alive is pretty amazing.

RF: And he has his head together.

ROLLINS: He's got a grip on things, that's why he means so much to me. Because he's been through more hell than any human being I know. And he is intact. He's been through heroin, alcohol, hospital, TB, he is scarred. He is very fucked up. But he emerged from all of it absolutely intact. Hell, the doctors have told him that he has only a few months to live so many times, he must have a running dialogue with Death.

RF: Shining?

ROLLINS: Well, his body is cut up but his head is intact. He walks a bit funny because he has been cut up, all the ribs they cut out of him, but his eyes are intense all the time, always looking right through you. He doesn't hold back, if you ask him a question if he knows the answer, he'll tell you. Like: Hey Selby tell me about when you got busted with heroin and the cop put the gun to your head and you detoxed in jail with a bunch of drag queens, and he will look you in the eye and tell you without holding anything back. I like people who don't fuck around. And he doesn't make any big deal about it. He is not a celebrity. He lives in a small apartment with his birds and that's it. If more people had that kind of honesty and strength, things would be a lot cooler around here.

RF: You probably meet one person like that in a lifetime.

ROLLINS: I don't meet many people at all, Ok, I talk to a lot of folks, and a lot of people talk to me, but very rarely do they say anything to me. I don't meet a lot of people that I remember.

RF: Does that have to do with your relationship with your father?

ROLLINS: No, it has to do with how I relate to people. I hear too many talking loud and saying nothing, usually if I have to meet one person a day, that's one person too much. I honestly do not like interacting with people very much. I don't like phone calls, I don't like letters, I don't like answering letters. I don't like making phone calls.

RF: Are interviews are more like a fair situation? It's a special kind of interaction.

ROLLINS: Most of the time, it's nothing more than business, you know. I make no bones about that. I will tell them the truth, I will tell them anything they want to know because I have nothing to hide. But it is the means to an end. I am getting in the newspaper. People will find out that I am playing and I can avoid the thing that I hate, and that is secret shows. A secret show is when you get to a town and you're in the record store checking it out and someone comes up to you and asks what you're doing there, you tell them that you're playing, and they had no idea, that's a secret show, there are secret records as well, that's where some one tells you that you should do an album someday, and you tell them that you have done a few and they have no idea because there's no real distribution. With the media, with the newspapers you can get the message out that you are coming and that's why I do interviews. Not to cut out little pictures of myself and paste them on the wall and walk around all egotistical. It's not that I am not flattered, you know. They won't interview you, they won't interview my mom, they want to interview me, and that's wild, man! That's cool. But it's just typeset and printed on paper. Big deal. I am not a very social person, I don't have a girlfriend nor do I want a girlfriend.

RF: How do you live ?

ROLLINS: I rent part of a small house in Los Angeles I got a small room. It's cool, there's a futon on the floor that a girl gave me years ago, shelves, a desk, stereo, a few books, a typewriter, a telephone, an answering machine. No big deal.

RF: Home sweet home?

ROLLINS: I like sparseness, I don't like piles of junk. Things I own are functional, the only luxuries I buy are coffee, records and books. I love music so I'm always in the record store looking at my last dollar debating if I should walk home instead of taking the bus and buy the record. I am addicted to music. That's where my extra money goes. But these days I am in a good position, because most of the bands I like, I get the records either from them or their record company. Some of the bands I like are on the same label as I am. I didn't buy many records on this tour, I can't afford them. I did buy a few: some Tom Verlaine records and a Chuck Brown record, I got Swans, Sonic Youth and stuff like that for free.

RF: How does the term "living like a monk" appeal to you?

ROLLINS: I don't know much about monks, they don't have much ?

RF: They don't have anything, they are very disciplined.

ROLLINS: Yeah, right on. See, I need to live like this in order for to do what I want to do. I am on a very tight budget. Like most independent musicians. Very low on money, very low on time. I have to be smarter than Eddie Van Halen. I have to be smarter than Mick Jagger. Because I have less leeway. I can't blow 50,000 dollars, I can't blow 5,000 dollars and I shouldn't blow 5 dollars. I have to make very careful decisions. When we went into the studio, there was no time to make up songs in there like Deep Purple, no! You gotta go into the studio and know your material, that's all there's time for on our budget, it's wham bam thanks for the master tape ma'am. That's the way we have to work. We are on a budget, we are on a schedule. And that's it, and that's Ok, I can deal with that. I have been a lot poorer than I am now. I have lived in squalor, for years with Black Flag, we had some pretty lean times. We were eating maybe once or twice a day and didn't know where the next meal was coming from. And those were some very tense and aggravating times. I am living much better now, not leaps and bounds better. But, last year I had much more money and flexibility and freedom and time to myself than right now. Right now, I am pretty much up against it. I am in debt, I've got lots of projects. In order to realize what I am trying to do, I will not be able to stop working until at least October-November 1988. That will be the next time when I will be able to take six weeks and do nothing but write and catch up on reading and whatever. I will be six weeks in LA from tomorrow on, if I catch my plane but I have a lot of work to do. I decided to give myself Saturday and Sunday to cool out a bit. That will give me good incentive to get to work during the week. So on Saturday and Sunday I can write and read and listen to music, and take the phone off the hook, I can't do that during the week. But on the weekend, boy, I disconnect that phone.

I have no problems working the way I do, it's real, and I enjoy the tension. I don't think that much good stuff comes out of relaxed, well-fed, comfortable situations, I think you always have to be pushing, otherwise well, you are what you eat, and everything you do reflects where you come from. And things to me, that come from wealth and comfort and security. I am not interested in. Because I know where that mentality is at, and I'm not interested in that mentality. You have a different value system, Ok. And, personally I am not interested in that value system. I am not interested in peace and love.

RF: How do you do your writing, you obviously do a lot of it on the road.

ROLLINS: Right. That's where I do my best work. But usually, at the home-base, I have a typewriter and I have note-pads around. There's note-pad down on the floor near my bed I put there before I go to sleep, because late at night I wake up with an idea. Or I will be typing something, I come up with a very concise idea at the same time, so I write it by hand on the paper. I write it down very quickly and then go back to the type writer. I usually have paper on the left and the right of the typewriter. I try to write every day. I have written every day for over 158 days now, I do a lot of the shorter things on the typewriter, I bang it out. I get a real thing going. With the journal writing, since I am not a good typer, I like to use the hand. I can get the ideas down quicker onto paper.

RF: So it is not that you're sending home your notebooks and having somebody type it.

ROLLINS: Yeah, that too. That is the journal thing. The person takes the notebooks, goes through it and types it. I'm working on a few different things. I have projects that will take years to complete. There's a thing I have been working on for about year, called "Mekanik". It's a series of paragraphs, from my thoughts, from things I see, conversations I hear, I put down two or three of these paragraphs a day. And there is a file in the computer for Mekanik. So the typers, and we have hired different people, they go through the notebook. They first go through the Journal, then they put in Mekanik. They keep adding into the files, at some point I will make a print out and see what it looks like.

RF: In the reading shows, more than half of it is improvised.

ROLLINS: Yes.

RF: You are going write that down too?

ROLLINS: I have been trying to take care of that with records. The first one just came out in America a couple of weeks ago. I'd like to do two a year. I do a lot of stuff with the talking thing that never makes it in print, long monologues that never get into print, it's not really the reading thing. It's more the thing you can hear. I want to put out those records at a very cheap price so it's more like buying a magazine that talks to you, you hear it a couple of times and you give it away.

RF: Did you start with the writing before you started with the singing?

ROLLINS: Yes. I don't consider myself a writer, nor do I consider myself a singer or a musician. I'm not trying to say that I'm some mystic, obscure piece of furniture, it's just that, you read Celine, Selby, Nietzsche. That's writing. Ok? Not me, I just got stuff coming out of me. And I am crass enough to press it up into a book and sell it. If that makes me a writer to some, well ok. I refuse to get that orthodox with it. I do some records, I do some books. I do shows where I talk, I do shows where I scream into a microphone with a band.

RF: With the ethics of punk it became apparent that you didn't have to be a brilliant instrumentalist to go up on a stage.

ROLLINS: Sure, and in a way, I think, that's cool. You don't have to be Led Zeppelin, you don't have to stay in your garage, you can get up there if you have the motivation. That's an opportunity for people to do what they want. I'm all for that. But what I'm not into are people who don't try to aspire to something that is unique and excellent. I don't like people playing badly and still doing it because punk rock says it's ok.

RF: They'll get weeded out.

ROLLINS: Yes, they'll get weeded out. But I think it takes much too long. But ok, anything that people want to do that's not harming me that's fine. I have freedom of choice, I don't have to buy a record if I don't want to. I don't have to go and see that band play. That's fine, if they enjoy themselves. I aspire to excellence. With my writing, with the singing. For me, words are tools to get to feelings, to get to emotions, to get to the way I am. Words to me are clumsy. It's like trying to cut down a tree with a spoon. Those who can use words, who can make them hit like hammers and cut like sharp knives, I have a lot of admiration for them. That, for me, is true writing. I think I am getting better, when I look at my newer stuff, I say "Yeah, that's getting there", and with the music I am always aspiring to be clearer and more powerful and more me. It's hard to be yourself. It's something you become better at by doing.

RF: Words are tools and you have to use them in order to learn how to use them properly. You have to write in order to become a writer.

ROLLINS: Damn, I wish I had said that, yes, and that's why I usually don't like to get into discussions about writing. If someone wants to be a writer, I say shut up and write. Why are you sitting here talking to me, you should be at home or in a room or in a jail cell or in a hole in the ground with a note pad or a type writer or a crayon, doing it. You shouldn't be talking about doing it because you're wasting your time. Poetry workshops, I think that's just such shit. Courses on writing, I don't understand. They learn to do someone else's trip. I mean, I can be reading a book and appreciate that guy's trip. Sure. But I don't want to write like that guy. I can get off on the guys energy or the guys structure. Mostly what I am looking for in my writing and in the writing of those books and texts I read is energy. Energy in the lines. Energy between the words. Sentences that are fully constructed. Separate sentences inside a paragraph inside a page inside a book. Maybe there's only 5000 sentences in a book. 5000 real sentences with beginnings and ends like songs. Like Black Sabbath songs. Each song is like an epic. And you can do that with ten words, you can do that with five words, read Nietzsche, Selby. Good books pull you through them. Your head falls to the page, ok? I don't think I can do that yet, I'm trying. People write books for different reasons than the need to get something that is inside of them, out. That's why I do music, that's why I do books. That's why I lose sleep, something is in me and if I don't get it out of me, it will destroy me. Luckily for me, I have found music and writing as avenues to vent this energy.

If I didn't have the good luck to have found these avenues for letting off steam, I would be in a very bad state. I know how I was before I was writing and doing a band full time. I remember how I was. I was extremely violent, extremely hateful, full of self-hatred. I hated life. Because there was so much energy, I have a lot of energy in me, and before it went out in a positive way, like a rock concert or a book, it went out in ways that got me fucked up. I would do a lot of violent shit. I am glad I cut down. I am not big and I am not strong or especially smart. I know that if you keep playing that game, you wind up with someone who plays it better than you. There's an amazing thing about trouble. It's so easy to find, and all you have to do is think a certain way, and carry yourself a certain way, and as much trouble as you want will find you, like a heat seeking missile. Just go try it sometime. I mean, don't, but believe me, you ask for trouble, you will get it. You'll meet someone who will rip your head off, put it in your knapsack and send you home. Without a doubt, there's always a bigger, meaner fish who can bite your balls off and hand them to you. I learned that and luckily I learned it in time, before it happened to me. I used to get into violent episodes and they were escalating and escalating, I was in an incident where this guy got his head smashed in with a baseball bat and later a friend of mine got his throat slashed. I said, that's it, end. I finally came to my senses and two weeks later I joined Black Flag, that could have been me catching that bat. It could have been me getting my throat slashed because I was in the same place as these people.

RF: Your writing is constructed like your lyrics, it has all these catch phrases, these punchlines in it.

ROLLINS: That is one of the ways I express myself, but some of the best ways of expression are not with words. That's why I scream a lot in the music I do. I don't need the words all the time, I need the sound, people pick up on a sound.

RF: Which is very convenient for audiences who don't understand English.

ROLLINS: Sure. A tone can be universal. A laugh is a laugh. When I hear Einsturzende Neubauten, I don't know the hell what Blixa saying. I can read the lyric sheets, they are in English, I like the tone, the emotion that these sounds give off. Like a dog barking, there is an excited bark, a warning bark, I think that is true with human voices too. That's why I think that the music I do works in places where English isn't the first language. People can dig the intent, the force, the intensity, the emotion.

RF: In the 60's there were a few records, they called it "Jazz and Poetry", Mingus did one called "Scenes of the City", a combination of music and literature that has disappeared since then. I think that one of the purposes of folk music, of the "urban electric folk music" Rock and Roll, is to tell a story. R'n'R has lost that function. It disappeared in the 60's.

ROLLINS: I think it disappeared with the onset of advanced communication. I am into information but I try to stay away from all this communication networking, I think it waters things down. That's why I always have to go back and break it all down. No band, no music, just me talking. That's why I like to do these shows by myself, no band to hide some embarrassing words, some subjects you can just rock out with nothing like that. One guy standing there, ripping his guts out in front of you. There's very little real communication going on today. Henry Miller, there's a quote from his book, "The Air Conditioned Nightmare", something like: "We don't talk to each other. We merely regurgitate facts and figures gleaned from cursory glances at books and magazines". We are just like computers spitting gathered facts at each other. I go: "40 56 29" and you go: "The rain in Spain falls mainly on the plain". There's been no real human exchange in that. It's more like: Hey, you read the news today? -Yeah. So, now on the bus, going to school, going to work, what you have in common with your neighbor is Channel 7. The TV-Special that 9 million viewers tapped into the night before, that's what we can talk about. We can talk about Sylvester Stallone, Madonna, we can talk about things that don't matter to us, that don't have anything to do with us, that aren't even related to anything. That's what is known these days as conversation, communication.

I think there's a lack of someone in the public eye going to the front and pulls his pants down. That's why I can't stand pop-music. It bores me. It's like a hand job. To a certain extent it's ok. ZZ Top, sure, they've got a good thing going and they're rocking out talking about a woman or a car, that's cool. Ok, I can deal with it. But as far as getting communication out of this, there's not really much happening, and bands with a message, aah, come on! I just generalize, but a band like U2, like the Alarm, like Bruce Springsteen. Let's sit down and write a set of lyrics like "War is Bad", "Death Sucks", "Two and Two is Four", "In Wintertime it's Cold". All stuff that is politically correct, like all these bands in America that go: "Hey guys, it sucks. You guys had to pay money to get in here tonight" to the crowd. He didn't say anything to you. He milked your dick. I got no time for that. I am not saying that I have some big brilliant solution. But I'm not enthralled by handjobs. I do it myself, I don't need some stranger jerking me off thank you. That's why I do what I do. And I do it the way I do it. I am very serious about what I do. Yet, I don't take myself too seriously, I mean, I am the first to laugh at myself. And say: "Ah come on, Rollins, you're acting like an old woman". Fine, but I do take what I do very seriously. I mean, it's all I've got, and it's all I want.

RF: So, this is a consequence of the communication age.

ROLLINS: Yes, definitely. They asked Bukowski in an interview I saw on a video: "Do you think there's going to be more geniuses as time goes on or less". He goes: "Less". Why? He says:"Communication". There is a brilliant point made. You can turn on the TV and everyone is watching the same channel. Turn on the radio and everyone is hearing the same song. Everyone knows the same set of information, he said something like: you want a genius? Take a kid, beat the shit out of him and lock him in a room. And then you'll get a genius. I agree that there's so much communication that we all know the same stuff. You have millions of people all buying the same record. But, no, don't beat the kid, don't lock him in his room. Please don't do that. But I see what he means. Like, you want to really know something. Get down the way Zarathustra got down. Go onto the mountain and let your wisdom and your knowledge become so heavy inside you that you feel impelled to go to the people and get it out of you because your knowledge and your wisdom is making you stupid and blind. I am no genius, I have no lightning bolts of wisdom or inspiration, but I feel the need to get what is in me, out of me, I do it in public, it's not good enough for me to do it alone in my room. I must suffer from some kind of insecurity or ego-mania, I don't know what it is. But it's not good enough for me to write a book full of stuff and put it on a shelf, to be in a band and play in a garage, I have to go out and flaunt it. I have to inflict it live, on you, on me. Any chance I get. I feel absolutely, one hundred percent compelled to do this. Obviously it is not for the prestige, it certainly isn't for the women. In that way, I am absolutely on fire. All the time. I burn with the desire to get out.

RF: So, for yourself, you avoid the media-overkill completely.

ROLLINS: I avoid it as much as I can, because I know who is creating it and I know why it is being created. Who is creating it, those who have money and want more. Everything in the media these days is an ad for something, in my opinion, even the evening news is an advertisement. And now there's people advertising life-styles, large companies advertising fucking life-styles! And isn't it great that these companies also own the things you need to maintain this life-style. Marlboro doesn't sell cigarettes, they sell a picture of a girl and a car and a guy lighting a cigarette for her. Ok, would it surprise you if they had a hand in Ford, in Jack Daniels, in sports-wear, motorboats? They're all in the ad. A half-hour sit-com on television is robbery. You turn that on and someone comes in and hooks your dick up to the TV and milks the blood right out of it for half an hour. You got your brain and your soul sucked out of you for half an hour with absolutely nothing in return, stupid humor, just handjobs, it keeps your brain in neutral, it keeps you out of gear so when 9 AM. comes the next day, and you've got to get back in line at your sado-masochistic 9-to-6 job that you hate, and when you come home from work at 8 o'clock, when you're sure to be home, boom, you get the Michelob ad, the Budweiser ad and then the show which has a little bit of that sexual intrigue and enough explosions and gunfire and enough commercials to keep your mind geared to nowhere. By 11 o'clock, you've had a couple of beers, you're a bit tired and you have to get up and do it again in a few hours. They have you, they had you all day and they have you at home as well, they never let you go with the bullshit parade, with the relentless onslaught of shit and poison. If you believed it all you would be dead by age 25 and you would still be able to get to work on time.

RF: And the whole soft-drugs business and pot is about the same thing.

ROLLINS: Drugs are legal in America, they're illegal but they're permitted. If Ronald Reagan didn't want people to smoke dope, do you think for a minute they couldn't spray the pot crops in

Northern California, which is the finest pot in the USA, and owned by guys who patrol their fenced areas with shotguns, it's their property, it's their pot and you don't touch their pot, I wouldn't touch their pot because I'd have a hole shot through me. When the cops come, these guys start to shoot at them. It's their property, the cops go away. You can put a man on the moon, you can slaughter thousands of men and defoliate half of Vietnam but you can't decimate a batch of green vegetation? Bullshit. I'm not saying that is what I would want to do, but if you want to get rid of pot in the USA you could do it. The government and the police like drugs, drugs are great for police work. With drugs, youth in the ghettos can keep on killing each other and the pigs get more time to spend eating donuts and drinking coffee. Drugs are great, anyone caught with them is a "criminal", and the pigs get to kick the shit out of criminals, it keeps all the stores open and all the lights on. Crime is good business, like war. I'm not for or against pot, I'm just saying that drugs are legal. Drugs make people a lot of money, in America, that's what it's all about, it doesn't matter who is buying them, if 10 years olds are getting addicted to shit, if it makes someone money, then there will always be a way to get what you need. The government makes money off drugs, private enterprises make money off drugs, the Mafia makes money off drugs. That's why drugs are legal, the people who make the laws protect their own interests. Marijuana is California's biggest cash crop, bigger than corn and tomatoes, bigger than love. The most hideous poison in the world, alcohol, is not only legal, it's glorified. It's a life style. You buy the lifestyle when you buy the brew. Alcohol is poison man, it rips your body to shreds, it screws up your internal organs. I came up with this warning label to put on the liquor bottles, there is a law that obliges people to put the ingredients on foodstuff labels. But look at a Jack Daniels bottle, you won't see any ingredients listed there. When you buy glue to make a model, the container says: Warning! Do not inhale, flammable, keep out of children, do not ingest this stuff. Ok. And now Jack Daniels, something that makes you have false sense of security, "Oh, I can drive!" Why don't they say on the side of the bottle: "Taken in the wrong amount, this can cause a false sense of security, false sense of awareness. This liquid has the potential to destroy your life, your internal organs, your work and your family, your life. Keep this out of the way of your kids. Not to be sold to minors". They don't say anything like that. No man, it's just cash and carry. Party down. Have a drink, son, you just turned 18, have your first beer on me. Welcome to the club. Welcome to Death City. I hate alcohol, I hate cigarettes, I hate pot, I hate drugs. I do have an opinion on them. I hate them. But I'm not going to slap your drink out of your hand, I'm not going to slap the joint out of your mouth. But man, 7 year old kids smoking pot and getting their minds fucked up...pot is not harmless, alcohol is not harmless, cigarettes are not harmless. They fuck you up. There are people who are campaigning for legalization of marijuana, I'm not into that. Though I think it should not be considered a crime. It is just a fucking joint, but it's not harmless. On pot, people don't function. Hey I could be wrong, whatever smoke that dope, shoot your shit, there will always be AA, NA, places you can go and sit with a bunch of fucked up people like yourself and you can talk about drugs and booze and how much you don't do it anymore. The truth is when you're fucked up, you're a fuck up, you don't have a chance out there. America is a killing machine. The money-makers have found a ways to kill you slowly so they get maximum money and maximum work out of you, they will keep you on the planet until you're about 65, and in that time they've milked your blood out of your dick, they sold you life-styles, they sold you values that don't exist for you, that don't benefit you, they only exist on color photographs. The companies who run things want to kill you. They are murderers. They don't like you. They hate you. I say, don't be a sucker. Be aware. Open your eyes. You better get your discipline down. You better have a loaded gun. You better start walking the street with your eyes open. You better start listening to what is in the wind, otherwise, you're going to be one of these people who gets used. The time to wake up is now. The big brother trip is all around you. It's 360 degree paranoia all the time all around you. It is time to have eyes all the way around your head. To be a total awareness unit. You've got to be relaxed, balanced and aware at all times. Because, man, someone who's got lots of money, lots of time, who puts incredible, brilliant minds to the task of ripping you off and making you conform. It is a long term project, it takes a lifetime, yours.

RF: The main tools of this manipulation and control trip is the media.

ROLLINS: I would agree.

RF: But you are, and I am in this same business. We use paper to print our words.

ROLLINS: But I know my intent.

RF: You said before that you wouldn't buy a TV?

ROLLINS: Well...

RF: But you would buy a monitor and a video?

ROLLINS: I might do that.

RF: Something you can control yourself?

ROLLINS: Yes.

RF: So, where do you draw the line, I mean, in the Rock Biz, and even if it's a complete alternative, there's just as much sucking as in the whole corporate biz.

ROLLINS: Today, there hardly such thing as alternative music. There's not many truly alternative labels. A lot of American independent labels are nothing more than launch pads for the major labels. The major labels are gleaning from the small ones. They watch the independent bands as they drive their vans to every shitty, stinking club in America, when one of them shows some promise, a major will snap them up. Independent labels are like farm teams for the majors. When Warner Bros. comes knocking with a truck full of money, it's not a matter of integrity to say no, bands know that with a major they are going to get far more exposure and money than with an independent label, there's nothing wrong with that, what sucks is that these indie labels get no respect, they have to work harder and smarter than any major to get their bands out on the road and into the stores. These bands and labels work until they just about drop and then some smooth fuck from way up on high comes along and gives them a tap on the shoulder, what a lot of these small bands that are getting signed don't know is how long they will tickle the fancy of the major that signs them. When you do a record on a major, and it stiffs, you can get lost in a pile of paperwork on someone's desk, you will wish you were back on that independent label. Major labels can waste your time, they have a lot of power, they can make you wait, they can keep you from working, sometimes these bands get really fucked over. I'm not going to name names, but I've seen things and heard some real nightmare stories from these bands, whatever. I hate it when I hear about a band getting run over by the label they are on, big or small, you only go around once, it's a shame to have your life wasted by someone that isn't you, by someone that really doesn't give a fuck about you.

RF: You don't have much in the way of personal belongings.

ROLLINS: The less you possess, the less that possesses you, I believe in that.

RF: So you can't be corrupted.

ROLLINS: Yeah. And it's easy to get corrupted. And that's why a lot of bands like Bon Jovi, they are big in America. I am sure Mr. Jovi is a nice guy, you know, three years ago he was cleaning the ashtrays in a recording studio. I am sure he knows everything about being hungry. Now he has got millions of people, literally, saying: You are the greatest. Girls throwing themselves at him. He's not travelling in a used car anymore, he's not taking the bus anymore, he isn't staying in someone's apartment on the floor. He's staying in a four star hotel, he's not carrying around his own equipment, he's playing to 18-20,000 people a night. I do a whole tour and don't get to that many people, he does that in one night. Mr. Jovi gives away more records to the press than I sell. Now, you surround a nice kid from New Jersey with something like that, what the fuck do you think is going to happen? He is not made out of steel, he is made out of flesh and blood like you and I. I am sure that he has a different attitude from when he started, I am not playing for peanuts anymore myself, I am not playing for just enough money to put some gas in the car anymore, I used to do that. I used to play just for the gas. Now I got a fucking beautiful theater to play in tonight and they bring me coffee, I have a hotel room and I'm taking the plane home. I have come to certain standards myself, but I am very careful.

RF: Without possessions and without being corrupted, how long has this been going on?

ROLLINS: It's been six years straight.

RF: And how about love in these years?

ROLLINS: I was in love with a girl a few years ago. I love you and oh, I love you too, really, that's nice. I did that, I did my love trip. I no longer believe in that. I have admiration and respect and for some women I have a physical attraction. Like a lot of people. Love? Fuck that shit. Forget it, I am not interested, thank you. You can do it if you want. I've got places to be. I don't want anyone loving me. I don't even want friends. I don't need the responsibility. Partners, fellow celebrants in the harvest, fellow creators, yes. Peers, people I can see eye to eye, people I can respect. That's what I want, and as far as interaction with a female goes, it's hard for me to find a girl that I can be with. I can only be with a girl I can respect. I can't deal with women I can't respect. And I can't find women which I feel are on par with me. I'm not saying that I'm some kind of big icon up in the sky. Every girl I've gone out with freaks out when we are somewhere and someone comes up to me for an autograph, or hustles for an interview. Or when I walk up on stage and people start clapping and calling my name. And then there's the schedule, I am never around in one place more than a few days at the most, like some girl wants to hang out with a guy that's home

6 weeks a year, I've tried it before and it always comes out the same way, the road always wins, you do this kind of thing full time, there are certain things you go without. This girl I used to go out with for a long time was very jealous, she couldn't take it that I people know me in a public place. I told her: Don't you understand, these people are cool, they're just checking in, at the end of the night, we go home and here is your man. She couldn't handle. It alienated me and made me understand some things. Love is different for everyone. A lot of people love me, Ha! And I'm all over the place, hated, liked, admired, respected, unknown. Love to me is not important. Respect is important. Equality. And that's why I filter all my human contacts. People I can respect, that's what I want. I'd like to find a woman I can respect. One that blows me away. The Uber-Woman. I want a new species. Someone who can say Hi, I am so busy that I have barely a moment to acknowledge you at all, you're a nice guy, see you in a few weeks, I have to go. My heart would come out of my mouth for someone like that. I thought I met a girl like that a year ago, I thought I had finally met a girl that didn't have time for me, I was wild about her. It was just so awesome, but it burned out. But I like women, man. I'm a big fan of women. I like the way they look, I like the way they think, I like the way they smell, I like the way they feel, I like the way all the parts move, I think the female is the most awesome machine on earth. There's nothing I admire more than a woman that is in shape. It makes me go wild. More than anything, except maybe for playing. The most beautiful thing I've ever seen is the female form, without a doubt. It's frustrating to not be able to connect. To know that the parts aren't compatible.

RF: Yeah, what's inside a girl?

ROLLINS: See, that's the thing. That's what a lot of people look for, some kind of magic thing inside their partner. And that's something I don't like about love. Because love hurts people and I don't like people getting hurt like that. "Love is based on something larger than life" "Love will get us through" No man, you're the one that gets you through, biology looms too large in my mind to accept the idea of love right now, maybe when I'm older and more mature, aren't I funny.

RF: The mechanism also applies to the relation of parents to their kids. All these frustrated mothers who put it on their little son.

ROLLINS: Yes. Anything you don't get, you will give the negative of it to your kid. Your man doesn't love you? No problem, just pass the hatred onto your kid. Single mother, frustrated, can't get laid as much as she wants to, so she smacks the kid. She can't pick up a guy at work, can't meet up with a guy at a bar and have a normal sexual relationship for a month. "Goddamn you piece of shit kid, if I didn't have you I could go out and have a normal life". That was the rap I was given when I was young. "You're a pain in my ass". Now I am a pain in her ass? Fuck that, did I ask to be here, can I go out and get a job and drive car? No! I am fucking six years old, man. Ha! Give me a break, I am just the one who uses the toilet, man! So many kids can't deal with it even when they are 16, let alone when they are seven. These are the real horror stories. It's not "Friday the 13th". It's not 'Nightmare on Elm Street". No man, it's the nightmare going on next door to your house. When I think about kids getting hurt and abused by their parents, it makes me just absolutely fucking crazed. That's when I go physical and destroy. I hate parents. Parents are the downfall of man. Hahaha! Certainly the biggest problem for kids are parents. I think there should be more care put into the handling of kids.

RF: I recently saw a video about kids in a penitentiary in the States, they are about 15 or 16 years old and most of their fathers are Viet Vets.

ROLLINS: Yeah. The father comes back psychically damaged without little or no government help to try to get his mind back together. It's inconceivable to you and to me, being in the jungle and watching your buddy exploding next to you, of having his brains on your face, and a few days later you're back in America and your is wife getting angry because you're late coming home from the store, she has no idea what has happened to you. There are thousands of men who came back so fucked up. And they were just kids from the mid-West, 17-18 years old, one month they're trying to get laid and working and hanging out with their friends from school and months later they're in the jungle. And it's not like WWII, when we were "fighting the enemy" for "patriotic" reasons. No, it's an unseen enemy. You don't know really why you are there, the lines were never clearly drawn. The conditions were much more hectic. The people know a lot more about the way things go and a lot less about why they were there. And they come back and they feel that they were ripped off and used. They were used for cannon fodder. These people came back after spending a year in country, having done things to strangers that they never would have believed they would have ever done, they have no way to reconcile it, they live an entire life with this "crime" on their shoulders, imagine being one of the men that was at My Lai, imagine the karma that carries. These men and women were sold out by a bunch of fat fucks that never got out of the sand box. Can you imagine a man insane enough to order 50,000 humans into slaughter at one time with a few phone calls? Can you entertain the notion of something like that? Someone like that should be taken out of circulation! And this war was so different from any other fucking war. The way people came home, they came back to a government that said: "War? Oh yes, you're a little upset about going over there and trying to go back to being a farmer without your legs. Well, we are sorry about that. That's really horrible. Ok. Well, good luck buddy !" The guy gets off the plane and then a hippie girl comes up and spits in his face, calling him a baby killer. I went to school with teachers who were in Vietnam and I heard all kinds of stories. Years ago I knew a man named Rocky, he was a local nutcase. One day we were hanging out at Guy Mason ball park on Wisconsin avenue. He was drunk and he told me this story about how he bayonetted a kid out its mothers arms and threw it over his shoulder. He was telling me all this and then he starts freaking out, screaming and crying, he started strangling me, I nearly passed out before I got loose, he was out of his mind. I had bruises on my neck for a week. The problem in America is that people make big messes around them and they don't clean them up. They ignore the mess. That's the American way. I think they call it "progress" or something like that. That's how Americans are in Europe. They leave places like a child leaves a room. "Someone will take care of it". This happens on all levels. That's the reason why I don't want to appeal to the mainstream, why I don't want to work on a broad level. The masses are fucked and always will be terrifying because they believe. One of the masses deserves everything that's coming to him. There is as much information as you need available to you these days. Ignorance is no excuse. Frank Zappa made a great point in an interview I read recently, he said that the standard of excellence is mediocre in America. People strive for mediocrity, they aim for it. Imagine a guy in a studio going for mediocre music, imagine aiming your life for the middle of the road. That's evil, man. The sheep get slaughtered. They get ripped off, pushed around, manipulated, they get turned into slaves.

RF: And things are going to become worse.

ROLLINS: Yes they are. The whole trip is now swinging to the right in America. You'll get more censorship, more clamp down, I'm sure that eventually I will get fucked with, my books will get busted. I am sure they will eventually read my fuck-you pig stuff. I am now in that frame of mind, it's not good times, it's not Coney Island, it's not a fucking disco. It's fucking war. Now. That's why I relate to the military thing. I relate to discipline because that's what's going to get us through. An artist in the next ten years is not going to be this kind of irresponsible dreamer, there's no more time for that comfort factor. No man, he's got to be smart, to provide a field where people can get some righteousness. You have to be really smart. It's not going to be easy to get shows in the future. In the next three years being on the road in America, I bet it will be hard for me to get shows. A lot of the small clubs are closing up. You will have either very small places or you'll have to be as big as REM. A 600 seater like the Rote Fabrik in Zurich, which is the perfect size for a lot of bands, places like these are drying up. Now, the line has been drawn. The real poor or the real rich. The middle is climbing for higher ground, and if they have to climb over you, they will do it. And if you wake up one morning with a footprint on your face, you slept too long, you overslept! You've got to sleep with one eye open. Someone's going to move right in on you and move over you. And the more independent and the less you have your hand in the machine, the better. "I want a credit card", "I want a bank account". They got your ass on file. My mom, you know, I get these raps: "Oh son, you're so hard line". I take care of my mom's house for 3 days while she is away. In that time she will get so much junk mail, it's incredible, about 40 pieces of junk-mail, catalogues, buy this, buy this, buy this, you can use your credit card. How did they find her address? Because Master Charge sold their list of clients to them. They put the names in the computer, hit a button and the labels come out and they slap them on their catalogue and send it through, bulk mail. They don't even pay the full price, they pay a fraction of regular postage to send the stuff. Ok, so I said: Mom, you're killing me, telling me I'm too hard lined, too this and too that. And I say Ok, I can tell how full of shit you are by how much junk mail you get. How many asses you got your mouth hooked to is relative to the stack of junk mail in your house. Look how many people are sucking off you right now. Now don't tell me I'm full of shit, you got people disrespecting you all the time, trying to take your money and fucking suck your dick. They're just milking blood out of your dick. That's what I say to my mom and she starts with: You don't get it, you don't like me. Mom, I get that you're not seeing the whole thing. I want to get out man, anyone who gets in the boat is going to go down, I want out. I righteously want out. I'm a soldier for out.

RF: Where to?

ROLLINS: Where to? To me, to one. It's been branded into you, the social thing: Oh, you aren't going to the prom? What, are you some kind of weirdo? What's the matter with you, you don't have a date? Are you a queer? You better get yourself a date. What's the matter, you don't drink? You're some kind of faggot! You don't want to smoke pot? What, you're a wimp? No. I want to sit in my room by myself. God, you are a freak! Well, I don't want to get drunk and go to a football game and sit for half the day watching a bunch of guys running around a field. What, you're un-American? You're a commie. Maybe you're in the wrong country, pal! Fuck that shit, ok? So the people who jump on the boat are headed for the Big Death. Like the big house on Malibu with the sticks coming out of the bottom supporting it because it's built on a cliff, you know what's happening to that house? Everything is eroding. And suddenly, bye! And where do these people go? Chuck D. of Public Enemy always tells people that they got to know what time it is, Flavor Flav is out there with his big ass clock around his neck so you can see!

RF: You know what time it is!

ROLLINS: You know what time it is. Chuck said at the end of this interview: People GOT to know what time it is, and that gets it right. People got to know what time it is, I'm not into the political thing. It's just seeing it, you know. Seeing the big death. And mind you, we are heading back to the Lenny Bruce days. We are getting the full job for saying cocksucker, believe me! And that's why I am Part animal-Part machine. You got to deal with the fuckers. You can't be afraid if it's ugly, you can't crawl away. You have to look the lie right in the eye and not be afraid to see too clearly.